It's Complicated

(But It Doesn't Have to Be)

It's Complicated
(But It Doesn't Have to Be)

**A MODERN GUIDE TO FINDING
AND KEEPING LOVE**

PAUL CARRICK BRUNSON

GOTHAM BOOKS

GOTHAM BOOKS
Published by Penguin Group (USA) Inc.
375 Hudson Street, New York, New York 10014, U.S.A.
Penguin Group (Canada), 90 Eglinton Avenue East, Suite 700, Toronto, On-
tario M4P 2Y3, Canada (a division of Pearson Penguin Canada Inc.); Penguin
Books Ltd, 80 Strand, London WC2R 0RL, England; Penguin Ireland, 25 St
Stephen's Green, Dublin 2, Ireland (a division of Penguin Books Ltd); Penguin
Group (Australia), 707 Collins Street, Melbourne, Victoria 3008, Australia (a
division of Pearson Australia Group Pty Ltd); Penguin Books India Pvt Ltd, 11
Community Centre, Panchsheel Park, New Delhi – 110 017, India; Penguin
Group (NZ), 67 Apollo Drive, Rosedale, Auckland 0632, New Zealand (a di-
vision of Pearson New Zealand Ltd); Penguin Books, Rosebank Office Park,
181 Jan Smuts Avenue, Parktown North 2193, South Africa; Penguin China, B7
Jaiming Center, 27 East Third Ring Road North, Chaoyang District, Beijing
100020, China

Penguin Books Ltd, Registered Offices: 80 Strand, London WC2R 0RL, England

Published by Gotham Books, a member of Penguin Group (USA) Inc.

First printing, November 2012
10 9 8 7 6 5 4 3 2 1

Gotham Books and the skyscraper logo are trademarks of Penguin Group
(USA) Inc.

LIBRARY OF CONGRESS CATALOGING-IN-PUBLICATION DATA
has been applied for.

ISBN 978-1-592-40769-9

Printed in the United States of America
Set in Sabon
Designed by Spring Hoteling

While the author has made every effort to provide accurate telephone numbers,
Internet addresses, and other contact information at the time of publication,
neither the publisher nor the author assumes any responsibility for errors, or
for changes that occur after publication. Further, the publisher does not have
any control over and does not assume any responsibility for author or third-
party websites or their content.

Names and identifying characteristics of individuals mentioned have been
changed to protect their privacy.

My dear Kingston. I thank God each day for you. You changed my life the moment you came into this world. I dream for you to dream bigger and more audaciously than your mother and me. With this book, I hope to leave this place a little bit better for you than how I found it.

Contents

There Will Always Be Rules

Once, one of my favorite bloggers said he was at a discussion where a panelist boldly announced the only rule to dating is that there are no rules.

When he said this the audience erupted with applause. Heads nodded. The "amen" choruses began. But almost as soon as he made this statement, after a microsecond of thought, he reversed his stance and started to spout guidelines.

No matter what people say about dating in the twenty-first century—there will always be rules.

But this isn't your grandmother's dating scene.

Since the 1970s, marriage rates, for all Americans, have decreased by 50 percent. Why? For one, people are waiting longer to get married. According to a 2008 study by the National Marriage Project, since 1991 the average age for marrying has increased to 32 for American men and 29 for women. Of those people many are opting to live together before getting married. In 2000, more than 11 million Americans were living with an unmarried partner, ten times the amount of unmarried couples who lived together in the 1960s. Then in 2012, the population of unmarried adults versus married tipped ever slightly in the favor of the unmarried for the first time in history.

There was a time when it was normal to meet your future husband or wife while still in high school and marry him or her upon graduation. Men either went into the workforce or attended college. You didn't move very far from your family, and you didn't have to move very far for work. But society has changed.

You want to go to a better school? You want a better job? You want to make more money? You move to where that better education, that better job is. Our society is mobile, and work, career and education are often prioritized over marriage. Now, after college, most men and women are intent on paying off their student loans, not focusing on marriage. They're trying to build careers, not families.

What was the driving force behind dating in our parents' and grandparents' generations? Marriage. It wasn't about self-discovery or experimentation, or let's just play house and see how it feels. It was for finding someone to settle down with, to start a family and get serious.

There was no such thing as casual dating thirty years ago.

But the rules have changed. Adolescence no longer ends with your teens. People still call themselves "boys" and "girls" and claim "youthful indiscretion" for their mistakes in their midthirties. If forty is the new thirty, and thirty is the new twenty, then twenty is the new ten, and when marriage is broached you react to it just like a ten-year-old would, with a feeling of incomprehensibility, immaturity and incredulousness.

What? Me? Married? I'm just a kid.

Yet the government still recognizes you as an adult at eighteen—able to vote and to spend your entire life in prison for a capital crime offense. You want love someday and one day find yourself on the wrong side of thirty or forty and realize you want love right now. But the game has changed. It's all changed so quickly and so much we don't even know what game we're playing anymore.

We live in a world of choices. Choices infinite and vast. Choices to live where we want, go where we want, do what we want, and be with whomever we want. Never in human history have any people ever had more choices.

It only makes sense that it would be a little hard to make up your mind.

But if you're confused, society played a role in getting you there. We're taught to believe in the inevitability of love. That it'll just happen. That one day we'll walk into the right room and bells will ring, a choir will sing, and our long, dark single night will end, giving way to a bright new coupled day. But while this makes sense for the "happily ever afters" of our most popular romantic fiction, it doesn't make much sense in our practical lives.

Yet that's what we believe. We say there are no rules in love yet bind ourselves in the rules and expectations written for us by screenwriters and TV executives, poets and singers, our parents and our ancestors—believing in society's romantic myths rather than our modern-day realities. In that desire for once-in-a-lifetime happiness we find ourselves in an everlasting state of wanting and wondering. It's a setup: you're told constantly how love "should" happen, then feel underwhelmed when romance doesn't unfold with a glorious sound track and end with a fade-to-black. When the reality doesn't match your expectations, it creates the wanting and the bitterness that follows that wanting.

You wonder: *Why didn't I get what I was supposed to get when everyone says it's just supposed to happen? Why does it seem everyone has everything and I have nothing of what was supposed to come naturally?*

Especially when I followed the "rules."

She followed all the "rules," and he did exactly what his father told him to do. Even though those rules and his father's advice were all colored by the experiences of others' failures, of their disappointment in learning society's love myths weren't true, then imposing their jaded perspective on you.

The contradictions pile up like cars in a freeway accident.

Never make the first move, she was told. Never let your guard down, his father said. And don't want it too much. But remember you still need to want it enough. Your friends tell you the fastest way to find love is to stop looking for it. Then they tell you to join an online dating website. You're told you need to settle things right away once you start dating, find out everyone's intentions. But then you're told not to scare them away with your desire for closeness and intimacy. You're told to give over your heart completely and love without abandon. But that you can never really trust anyone because every man and woman is a Martian and Venusian stereotype you have to beat at their own game. How can you trust? Best friends, homeboys and relatives said the last thing you could do is trust anyone. Love is a game of constant chin-checking, snooping, accusations and recriminations. All emotions must be guarded, save for anger and disappointment. Love is a battlefield where you never let them see the truth in your eyes, because they'll only use it against you.

And you get so much information. On television. Online. And it's coming, changing all the time.

You're told to delay sex. Then you're told you need to put out more. You're told to go all out to impress on a first date. Then you're told to be more casual and just go for coffee. She texts. He doesn't. He likes instant messaging. She likes a phone call. She's intensely private. He relays every intimate detail about his dating life on his blog.

You go to the club with your girls and wonder why no man ever comes near. (Psst. It's because you rolled up in a club with a bunch of girls.) You go to the club with your boys and wonder why every girl you hit on turns you down. (Psst. It's because you hit on every . . . girl . . . in . . . the . . . club. And none of them could hear you over those thumping beats.)

Is everyone crazy? Is that why you're alone? Is everyone an angry mass of clingy, distant, withdrawn, too intense, abusive, controlling, unfaithful hot mess? Or are you those things and that's all you attract?

You're looking for love in all the wrong and right places, and you're getting frustrated wondering, *What are the rules?* Where is the method in this relationship madness?

Should a man always pay for the first date? What if you're just meeting for coffee? What if it's a blind date? What if the woman asked? Should the person who asked pay? After that first date, how soon should a man call back? Should a woman call? Does a text count? Does a message on Facebook count? Does a chat on instant messaging count?

In the past a woman never approached a man, and a man asked a woman's father for her hand in marriage. There were arrangements and there was the exchange of cattle. Today, people leave home at eighteen, start careers at twenty-two; parents are those people you visit during the holidays, and women own their own homes. So why are you still operating by a playbook written in 1955? This isn't *Mad Men*, this is the real world. When it comes to love and dating in real life and online, it's time the book of love got an upgrade.

There will always be rules, but the game has changed. Every situation has its own nuances, its own indefinable idiosyncrasies. Meaning, while it may have worked for your friend who met his future wife at Free Wing Night at the club, and they had sex on the first date—it doesn't mean it'll work for you. Societal shifts have altered the game permanently and we have to adapt to the field.

Have you adapted?

CHAPTER I

Marriage Isn't for Everyone

She had a list. And it was long.

He had to be tall, dark and handsome, educated, with money, and masculine, yet still maintain the sort of sensitivity where he'd let her have her way in the ways she wanted it to be her way.

But he couldn't be a pushover.

He needed to be a traditionalist who was a breadwinner and gentlemanly, but she had no interest in keeping a house or washing dishes. She had a career after all, and *that* was the priority. Children were a must, although it was apparent from the conversation she hadn't thought much deeper about her future progeny than what outfits they would wear and what names she would give them.

But like so many of us, she wanted it all. Yet where was he? Somehow in her myopic focus on school and work and the acquiring of things, he had not materialized. It seemed so strange—living in a time where you could google any answer, order groceries to be delivered to your house and balance your checkbooks, send a text and talk to your mother all at the same time on the same smartphone.

It just seemed like finding a husband should be easier. Wasn't there an app for that?

And it wasn't just her.

It was him too. He who had focused on degree after degree, designer suit after designer suit, party after party, and every latest electronic gadget. He always had so much fun with his boys, but he thought maybe it was time to settle down. So he looked for her "everywhere." The golf club. The country club. The dance club. Even five-cent wing night at the nightclub. And while he'd met some very attractive women, he hadn't met any who shared his values of honesty and dependability.

But everyone told him he was in the "prime of his life" and "so good-looking" and "could get any woman he wanted." And finding women was so easy for him. But finding *the* woman he actually wanted to spend more than one night with was a whole other ordeal. But why hadn't he found her? After all, he was dating the most attractive women he could find. They were all so young and pretty, yet none seemed to care about the things he cared about. They had nothing to talk about. They had nothing in common.

They were attractive and everyone said he should have been happy with that.

Yet he wasn't.

And yet he wanted a wife. Or at least he liked the idea of one. Especially one who was never any trouble, never complained, never wanted anything, was loving, supportive, happy, drama-free and drop-dead gorgeous.

Was that so much to ask? Was it so bad to want the "perfect" girl?

And I asked them all, my clients, *"So you want to get married?"*

And their eyes blinked and their mouths smiled, and many nodded in the affirmative that, yes, someday—whether five years or five minutes from now—they desired an "instant spouse." Could I deliver?

But could *they*?

You say you want to get married. And that's quaint. But do you even know what you're really asking for? Do you even know what marriage is?

Many people want to get married. More than two million people in the United States get married every year. And about one million people every year get divorced.

Some people think the divorce rate is a sign of the decay of society or gender equality, but I tend to think the divorce rate is high because people are told they're supposed to get married and not everyone is ready for it. People are told to get married but don't know what marriage is. People are told to get married but marry the wrong people.

Divorce was low in the past because once upon a time it was socially unacceptable to divorce, and if you married within a church, the church wouldn't grant permission. People didn't get worse. They were always this bad. There have always been people incapable of being monogamous. There have always been people who probably would have been better off single. There have always been people for whom marriage was not a viable option. Only now people get divorced rather than spend a lifetime in a marriage that is a bad fit, unhealthy or just an honest mistake.

But despite the gift (and burden) of choice, many of us have great misconceptions about marriage, and those misconceptions are what drive our divorce rates up and lead to marital disasters. Our misunderstanding of what marriage is causes us to make bad decisions about it—about whether it's right for us or if we are ready for it.

It starts with these skewed and much abused notions about marriage:

1. Being single is a sign of failure.

2. You're supposed to get married.

3. Your spouse is your "soul mate" and the primary key to your emotional well-being and happiness.

4. Marriage is the only answer to your "problem" of being single.

These notions are not good ways to start your "pursuit" of marriage. Largely because they don't take into account what marriage really is (and marriage goes beyond sexual attraction and romance and being in that near impossible to experience, all-the-time state of "happy"), these notions are unrealistic and play on fears rather than the positives of being married versus being single.

Let's start first with your "problem." *Your "singlehood" problem.*

Recently, 2010 U.S. Census data revealed that for the first time there are more "single" households than "married," with the marrieds coming in at 48 percent. The news was met with gasps and pearl-clutching. Rising income inequality was to blame, according to some. Others felt the stat was misleading, considering that most Americans are waiting until they are older to marry, but many Americans—at a rate of more than 80 percent in almost all demographics—eventually get married before they hit their fifties.

Still, single people are viewed as a problem in a world where marriage is the answer to the scourge of the never-married.

Being single is often treated—by certain singles and those overly invested in the lives of singles alike—as some sort of horrid disease. Its symptoms include a feeling of being "incomplete" and an eventual death from loneliness, plus the possible decay of society. But marriage isn't something that should be entered under threat of an unfulfilled life checklist or out of pressure to settle. It shouldn't be seen as something you're just "supposed" to do. Because for some—it isn't.

I know what you're thinking—*I thought I was reading a book that would help me not be single.* And you are. But the path to finding a partner begins with being honest about what you want, what marriage is and whether you're prepared for it. This book isn't for lofty notions and pleasant platitudes.

It's about getting real.

It is too important and too life-altering to be reduced to a Valentine's Day card greeting, Julia Roberts's smile in a friendly nineties romantic comedy and an hour-long episode of *Bridezillas*.

But why do you think you need to blindly flail your way into marriage whether you truly comprehend what it is? It's simple. Society told you to.

A thousand years' worth of society, in fact.

For centuries, marriages were arranged between property-owning families. In many countries they still are. Whether it's a country with a tradition of a dowry (where the bride's family has to pay a certain amount to the groom's family to marry their daughter off) or a bride price (where the groom and his family must pay the bride's family for her hand in marriage)—women were part of that "property" exchange.

It was like a business acquisition, only the business was the continuation of the family bloodline and a joining of community ties. It was about prosperity and wealth. For a man, getting married was a rite of passage into adulthood and a way to demonstrate his social standing or even wealth. For many women, it was the main determining factor of how their lives would turn out. A good marital match meant prosperity, potential happiness, an ideally peaceful or loving home. A bad match had the potential to go from socially or financially devastating to fatal.

And we still see remnants of this attitude today,

where women often feel a great societal pressure to marry, rooted in the past reality that marriage was a life or death decision and the number one determining factor in a woman's personal happiness.

Case in point: There are a multitude of bride magazines. I, so far, haven't seen anything similar for men dreaming of wedding vows. That's not to mean many men don't want to get married, but that's not how society set up our gendered views of marriage.

And those views are constantly evolving.

Why our Depression-era grandparents married is often different from why our baby boomer parents did, and it continues to be very different for those of us born after the 1970s.

When my grandparents were going through their courting stage, their views on what made the other "marriage material" was very utilitarian compared to how my wife, Jill, and I came to our decision to marry. My grandmother cared whether her husband was "able bodied" and "smart" enough to generate income. My grandfather cared whether his wife was "healthy" and "capable of managing a household," including the raising of children.

Love wasn't a question. It was more about tolerance.

And even with my parents, while the rules were less strict and whether they were "in love" played a factor, the emphasis was on role function. Who would do what and how and when.

Yet when my wife and I courted, role function was more a subconscious question. For us, our main emphasis was our attempt to evaluate whether we loved each other, and then to determine our compatibility out of that love.

And with the emphasis on love, our view and expectations of marriage have changed. Love, over the generations, has become the priority of many, more so than capability and role function. Love is the primary determining factor for many before they can even entertain marriage.

Which brings us to the notion of a "soul mate."

A "soul mate" sounds nice. Countless films and books hit us over the head with the trope. It's serendipity, it was simply meant to be, they're the one, the only. My first, my last, my everything. This notion that there is one person in the world meant for you and only you and all hope is lost if you never find this magical, *always bring me up, never bring me down* love. But it's also a completely contrived notion and wholly unrealistic, setting up multitudes of people for failure.

When idealized romance is favored in detriment of compatibility, you get the worst version of the "soul mate" idea. A "soul mate," after all, is about the expectation of romantic perfection—from horribly imperfect human beings.

"Soul mate" hints at never-ending happiness, never fighting, never having problems, never feeling lonely or tired or frustrated within your marriage. It turns the idea of marriage into Disneyland—and who doesn't want to go to Disneyland? There's food and rides and music and cartoon characters and hours upon hours of fun.

Just don't look behind the buildings on Main Street, USA, and learn that it's all a façade.

The "perfect" person is a façade. No one is perfect. Someone might be "perfect for you." But even the person who may be perfect for you will not be perfect. Perfection is an illusion and we can't spend our whole marriage in Disneyland. The honeymoon phase eventually ends. Your "soul mate" is a human. It's a commitment, not the Country Bear Jamboree.

Which finally brings us to: Marriage is the only answer to your "problem" of singledom.

"Jennifer" is one of my matchmaking clients who views her singledom as a problem—placing her high in the self-sabotaging category of having unrealistic expectations of herself, her partner and what marriage is.

Jennifer says she "believes" in traditional marriage roles but desires a "modern" marriage.

Jennifer is a paradox.

A common paradox but one all the same. This is an individual—male or female—who desires to treat marriage like a buffet where you pick and choose the parts of it you like and disregard the rest.

Jennifer is in her late thirties, very attractive, educated and from a very traditional Southern household where her mother managed things at home while her father dealt with work and income.

And her main challenge in her pursuit of marriage is that she is looking for a traditional man who will pay the bills, take care of her and support her with his "manly skills," while she has little interest in the "traditional" role of a woman in such relationships.

Meaning, she doesn't want to cook and lacks an interest in most domestic arts. When she meets "educated" men of her social standing, she often rejects them for not being "manly" enough.

Yet there is no interest in the property-based norms of a true traditional marriage. She wants the security of tradition but none of the control or domestic constraints. Her singledom is a problem she greatly desires to fix, but her expectations are rooted in a mixed message of modern independence and the same old gender-based marriage panic.

Even though we are no longer living in a hunter-gatherer society or during the reign of the Holy Roman Empire, views on marriage—especially relating to gender—die hard. If you are single and you're a woman and the thought of you being unattached, regardless of your age, fills you with panic, you are merely responding to the historical stress women have traditionally faced when it came to marriage.

There's a reason why Jane Austen novels are so fraught with anxiety over a woman making the right marital match. They were written in the early 1800s, shortly before the Victorian era began in Great Britain. During that time women were not considered full "persons." Women lost any and all property they brought into a marriage to their husbands and retained nothing if they were later divorced. Husbands had full legal control over the income of their wives. Following divorce, men typically retained custody of children.

All this largely meant that if you ended up in a bad marriage as a woman, you were screwed. And there were few to no opportunities for a woman who remained single.

When marriage is your primary option for societal advancement, it's only natural you'd become extremely fixated on it.

We still see signs of this today. Discussions of marriage (or lack of marriage) are still targeted toward women. It is women who often are the most vocal about their concern in finding a husband and having a successful marriage. And marriage is still heavily marketed to women, even though in the United States, most marriages happen out of an idealistic and romantic notion and not out of a necessary arrangement. Today, unlike their Victorian counterparts, women have the opportunity to seek their own level of financial security and happiness—with or without a husband.

But it makes little sense to apply this same sort of panic to our modern age, as it doesn't serve anyone—male or female. There should be no rush to make a match without thinking through one's desires, motivations and actions. Marriage is not a notion to rush into out of desperation or something to be taken lightly. It should not be treated as a cure to a disease-like singledom.

So marriage isn't to be treated as a fluffy never-ending high of candy-coated kisses and mind-blowing "honeymoon" sex, nor is marriage to be treated as the end all, be all, defining factor in your long-term happiness that without it you will be less than a person. Both these attitudes are wrong and do not reflect our current times.

If your goal is a successful marriage, you cannot negotiate that success from a position of panic, uncertainty and weakness. You cannot treat it as a fun park. Marriage is more than an end goal on life's checklist—it is a major decision that will often determine the quality of your life and will have a major impact on your personal happiness, prosperity and future.

But it is not the only determining factor of these things.

Marriage is not a new car. Or a promotion. Or nice house. Or a long, desired trip to France. It is not a song on the radio. It is not the final five minutes of *Coming to America*. It is a commitment of two people to live their lives as one. And it means this whether we're talking about marriage as an exchange of property, as it has been historically, or if we're talking about the romanticized, idealized, love-based monogamy of today.

Especially when no matter how you began at the altar, how you end is the same—joined together, for better or worse, typically living under one roof, *negotiating*.

So you have to decide—*do I want this?*

Do I want to work more diligently than ever in my life? Do I want to emotionally invest? Do I want to be held accountable for my actions by someone I can't hide my actions from? Do I want to check with someone else first before I (a) change careers; (b) move to a new place; (c) make a major purchase; (d) stay out after work; or (e) all of the above? Do I want to care about how someone's day was? Do I want to share? Do I want to start a family? Do I want to sometimes sacrifice my time or pleasure or needs or desires for someone else? Do I want to compromise?

If you are not interested in compromise, you may find marriage quite difficult to near impossible. Marriage—whether for today's love or yesterday's money—is about compromise. Even if it's a "traditional" marriage in the eyes of a male-centric patriarchy, there is even compromise in that, a bargain made and a bargain expected to be kept.

It doesn't matter if you have an "excuse" for why you think you shouldn't have to compromise. Perhaps you've been hurt and you find it hard to trust and that is why you need to check his cell phone every five minutes and why she has to keep a separate checking account.

But if you've been hurt and you can't trust—how can you marry? Can't compromise = Maybe you shouldn't marry.

And compromise can be as simple as "Are you and your partner on the same page regarding what your relationship is?" If you don't think monogamy is important, but your partner thinks monogamy is above all, you have to find a compromise. Sometimes that "compromise" is "maybe a polyamorous person shouldn't date/marry someone who expects monogamy." And then you have to accept that. Compromising means being honest with others and yourself about what you want out of a relationship.

So are you ready for compromise? Are you ready for it to not always be about you? (Sometimes, of course, it will be about you, but once you get married, that will no longer be 100 percent of the time "you.") Are you positive that you are not a serial monogamist, a serious "loner who likes it" who is only entertaining marriage because "society said so" or someone who struggles with the concept of monogamy in a world where your partners seem to almost always expect it? Are you positive that you aren't angry from past hurts, distracted by current burdens that keep you from having the emotional capacity to care for someone who is not you?

Do you have the capacity to compromise?

Now, if you determine that you struggle with the concept of so much compromise, this does not mean you're doomed to die alone. Quite the contrary, being honest about what you want is the first step to getting the kind of relationship and love that work best for you. Marriage is a beautiful thing when it goes well. It's admirable and a wonderful building block for a family. But it benefits no one for someone not suited for marriage to enter marriage. It does nothing for those unprepared for it to plunge in and hope the idea of compromise grows on them.

By being honest, you can avoid a lot of the heartaches and drama that come from living the life someone else expects of you or living a lie that will eventually blow up in your face. There's nothing wrong with accepting that you're not marriage material. But there is something wrong if you push that square peg into a round hole and expect marriage magic, if you allow panic and the invisible hand of society to guide you into a role you are either not prepared for or do not fit.

You do have options. How open you are to them depends on how strong the hold of "tradition" weighs on you.

More than 60 percent of marriages today began with "shacking up" first. Being unmarried and living together—while often discouraged by some if your goal is marriage (and there will be more on that later)—is a perfectly fine solution if you are not the marrying kind.

So does living separately (an ideal solution for those of you completely hostile to the extreme degree of compromise that goes into marriage and cohabitation). So does serial monogamy if you're ready to let go of the notion that there's only one person in the world for you. Perhaps for you love simply begins and ends over and over again, like making new friends or taking on new careers or moving to different cities. Love is an ever-evolving adventure with different co-captains.

Maybe you like the emotional commitment and

security of a steady relationship but need a lot of sexual variety? That's what open marriages are for.

But to do this, again, you have to be honest with yourself and those you date about what you want. And that is truly what this first chapter is about—letting go of society's expectations, your parents' expectations and what you "thought" you wanted, and seriously consider what you actually "need."

Ideally, you may desire marriage. Practically, something else might be a better fit.

So what is the right fit for you?

You want to get hitched someday (or today, depending on your mood), but are you even up for it? What are your responses to these statements? Do you find yourself agreeing or disagreeing?

1. My partner shouldn't have different political, religious or social views from my own. Their thinking differently makes me think less of them and question if I should be with them.

2. If my partner loses or gains weight, becomes depressed, falls ill or into financial burden I am willing to help within reason, as long as this situation doesn't persist. I feel that even though they're having a rough time that shouldn't mean my own needs should be ignored or neglected as a result. Especially if this is going to last weeks or months at a time.

3. Infidelity in marriage should always end in divorce, no matter what the situ-

ation is. I won't reward bad behavior or be made a fool.

4. My own space and time are valuable to me. I don't feel I should have to give them up to my partner if they want to do something that I don't find beneficial or interesting to me.

5. I shouldn't have to tell anyone where I'm going when I go out as long as I eventually come back at a reasonable time.

6. The only person I'm responsible for is me.

7. There should be only so much debating and negotiating. My partner and I are so close we should almost always be on the same page. If they didn't agree with me, that would upset me.

8. My partner must support my dreams and ambitions, even if they conflict with their own. I should be made the priority. I won't be with someone who can't understand that.

Are these statements true? If not, ask yourself why you feel that way. Marriage involves a lot of altruism.

While it is important for us to retain our identities within a marriage, joining with someone to share a life means just that—joining together to share a life. You're going from everything being about you to being about "us." Are you ready for that?

CHAPTER 2

Men and Women Are from Earth

If only love was like the movies. Like the ones where the frazzled heroine falls down a lot and finds out the jerky guy was just "broken inside" and all she needed to do to fix him was take off her glasses and shake out her ponytail. The kind where all the guy has to do is fight a dragon or defeat the bad guy and he's rewarded with his own camera-ready damsel in distress.

And then seven dwarfs sing you off as you two ride a horse into the sunset of your "happily ever after."

Beautiful. But not all that realistic.

The stories tell us that women should be sympathetic beauties and men should be transformed brutes. That women want husbands and babies. That men want to conquer the world (or at least the workplace) then get in some sex with the hot girl before the ultimate win. Yet we live in a world where some women want to run Fortune 500s and some men dream of being a dad and settling into a comfortable, loving home with a mate. Did their penises and vaginas not properly inform them that they are "different" due to their gender and are only supposed to want the set things society has laid out for them on the bed of life?

Do you know your gender is supposed to be your defining factor—not how you actually feel on the inside? Not!

And yet here we are pondering the reality that people are the same but different.

You are not a cookie-cutter person who can easily fit into one or two categories. So why do you think everyone else should be? How can you demand that those you date see "you" when all you see in those you date is a "type"? If you date based on stereotypes—ignoring emotional complexities, nuance and denying reality—you will get the "stereotypical" result.

Loneliness and complaining about said loneliness.

In the search for love you have to move beyond the societal negativity of "all men cheat" and "all women care about is money," and get to these fundamental truths.

1. Human nature trumps gender.

2. Your future significant other is a person—not a possession.

3. You cannot permanently hide your true nature.

In my friend Kayt Sukel's 2012 book *Dirty Minds* she writes that while men and women's brains are slightly different in how they develop, at our emotional core, we're not that dissimilar.

> "When we talk about sex differences in the brain, people want to go all 'Mars, Venus' on you. They want to take these results and try to spread males and females way apart on function and ability," said [Larry] Cahill. "It is not like that. When you are talking about sex influences on brain function, you may have two bell curves that are significantly different from one another in certain instances. But those bell curves are still overlapping."
>
> [Jill] Goldstein concurred. "There is more variability within a given sex than between sexes in cognitive behavior and the brain.

That is important. In fact, I always say it twice so that people really understand that," she said. "There is more variability observed between women than between women and men in both the size of different brain regions as well as the function."

Sukel's research found that while there are some differences, men and women's sexual desires, and thoughts on love and romance, shared more similarities than differences. It was more of a "PC versus Mac" difference, to borrow from Sukel's book, than a "Mars" and "Venus" dichotomy. Believing that women don't care about sexual pleasure or that men aren't interested in nurturing are dangerous thoughts that limit us and cause us to fall down the rabbit hole into stereotypical and often degrading "all men/all women" talk.

You know how that goes: All men cheat. All women want money. All men are rude. All women are temperamental. All men want is sex. All women want is to have babies. All men are jerks. All women are bitches—so act accordingly. All men want to be breadwinners. All women want to be rescued. All men are afraid of marriage. All women are obsessed with marriage.

Focusing on stereotypes is great—if you plan on dating a stereotype. If you plan on being with a one-dimensional person full of artificial personality traits, programmed by some great gender-assigning computer in the sky, stop reading this book and go out into the world to crash into people only to be disappointed by their nuances, differences and contradictions.

Stop saying "all." It can be really misleading. It can mean someone who wants children could date a person for years who has repeatedly said they don't want kids. Then, after marriage when he's ready to start a family, her eyes buck and her mouth is agape and she storms out and he wonders, "What's your problem! I thought all women wanted kids!"

Except the one you married, who told you repeatedly she did not.

Much has been made throughout history of "men do this" and "women do that" and it is true, there do appear to be marked differences between men and women; but men and women are human beings, and all human beings are only as good as their options.

Describing behavior as male or female is an oversimplification of something far more complex—the reality that adult people are an intricate mix of nature versus nurture with a large dollop of social conditioning.

People will say it's in a "man's nature" to not want to ever settle down. But as recently as the

1980s, that's what most men did. Rich, poor or middle class. Black, white or neither. Typically right out of high school or college—often unprompted. It was even desired. The hallmark of a successful man was to raise and support a family. The only difference between the man of the 1980s and the man of today is the shift of society, where due to a mix of economics and gender norms, it's more acceptable for there to be a delayed adolescence, sometimes lasting well into the mid- to late twenties. And who gets married when they're an adolescent? Marriage is seen as a very adult venture.

How many people do you know who are waiting to get married because they feel they need to finish an education and make more money?

What's the chance that this person is you—no matter your gender?

Statistics show in this age, where it is markedly more expensive to raise a family, where a man lacking a college education is typically a low wage earner with not much chance for mobility (thanks to a dearth of higher-paying manual-labor positions that were abundant in the postwar boom of the 1950s through early 1980s), your best bet to getting married, staying married and having a healthy relationship is a mix of money and education.

It made sense, in the 1950s, to get married when you were still broke because people were getting married when they were just starting out in the world—in their late teens and early twenties. You hadn't lived long enough yet to amass a nest egg or own a home. Stock options? Investments? Student debt? What was that? Your grandpa and father went to college while on the GI Bill. And if they didn't have that, their young brides worked to help put them through college.

This doesn't mean that the 1950s and 1960s were some marital paradise. It was easy to get into a marriage, but if it went badly it was hard to get out of, especially if you were a woman. And marriage was decidedly tilted toward men. The wives were working to put their husbands through college so they could be better wage earners. If the wives had any aspirations of their own, they were either put on hold or they never materialized because wives were expected to be helpmates and mothers—and to not have ambitions of their own.

But women—shock, shock—are human beings.

And this is the part where, as human beings, we are often only as good as our options.

As women gained more opportunities, it wasn't particularly surprising that marriage rates would go down. But just like professional equality is a work in progress, there is still a glass ceiling to break through for many when it comes to actual gender parity in heterosexual relationships.

We are still bound and tied to the old ways of thinking, those old beliefs based on the gender norms of a bygone era. A man is supposed to make all the money—even though she has a 401(k) and pulls down six figures. A woman's value is in her youth and fertility—even if many are delaying marriage into their thirties and beyond. All the reasons for why men and women appear to act differently but are much more alike comes down to both sexes reacting to decades of social gender norms that only have a 50-50 shot of actually coinciding with how people actually feel. This is why there are so many complaints of *gender expectation* not meeting *human reality*. Women aren't necessarily any more nurturing than men, but to be nurturing is expected of women and it's considered a valuable trait in a woman (especially if a woman is expected to be a helpmate wife and the primary child-caretaker). Men, even if they are actually nurturing and enjoy being that way, are told to suppress it or never develop that trait at all. (Which is another problem in a world where women tend to value a man who is supportive and complain that most of their relationships end because their significant others either could not or would not do the emotional work to further develop the bond.) But if you're a woman who actually isn't nurturing you're treated as some awful aberration. How many times have you read of men complaining of women who aren't soft, gentle, compliant, nurturing, supportive creatures? Women who bristle and complain, "I'm your girlfriend/wife, not your mother?" Who seem wholly unsympathetic? Who are indifferent mothers and inattentive wives?

Women often lament that the men of today don't seem to want to be "men" anymore. That they're overgrown "man-babies," disinterested in making enough money to support a family, searching for a mother they can have sex with who will do all the heavy emotional lifting (and occasionally all the heavy financial lifting). But how many of these men would be ideal "providers" if the shift from blue collar to white collar hadn't been so abrupt, if college had not become increasingly cost-prohibitive, if your student loan debt meant you took your first job while still living in your parents' house?

And who's going to date the guy who lives at home with his mom?

But how many men would date the girl who does?

And who made these rules? Centuries of social engineering where historically women were property of their families, didn't work, didn't go to school and lived at home until a husband was found.

The stigma is still the same, even if there's no use for it anymore.

A lot of getting over gender stereotypes is about

accepting that just as you aren't "the norm" many, many others aren't either. It's moving beyond seeing a person as a type but realizing that he or she is an individual with his or her own desires, wants and needs, independent of your own. And to have a healthy relationship, it means accepting this reality.

"Mark" came to me wanting an instant wife without the work.

A successful restaurateur, handsome and wealthy, he'd made his career his primary focus, wanting to farm out his search for a mate to me. He initially treated our sessions as if I were a dating concierge who would take his lists of desires and find him this dream woman who would never question him, be completely understanding about his demanding career, and give him an instant family.

But that's not a woman. That's a robot.

While someday in the future Mark might be able to purchase a female android programmed with the submissive personality type of his dreams, the Mark of today had to contend with the fact that even the most submissive woman is going to have some likes and dislikes. She's going to have some wants and desires.

And there will be something about her that will not fit the Stepford wife prototype of heels, pearls and easy sex.

Due to centuries of women being treated as property in marriages, there are many, many men (and now many modern women) who think of their future mates as simply extensions of themselves—like a new iPad or a nice leather couch. And when you see people as objects, you tend to get stuck in stereotypes.

Mark was looking for a possession when he first met me. He'd put no thoughts into what values his future bride should have. He just wanted "a bride," a bride who was a soft, agreeable woman, grateful for the comfort of his finances, and who would never ask too many questions.

Yet Mark had dated traditional homemaker types. The kind who desired to be helpmates. And they were attractive. And they were nice. And they were smart, but . . . he couldn't really tell who was serious and who just wanted her lifestyle financed.

Because the women Mark kept meeting saw *him* as a stereotype.

The handsome breadwinner.

So Mark juggled the women, charmed and flirted with them, treating each one of them the same, waiting for lightning bolts to strike. The women who might have been compatible with him became distrustful due to his indifference, and the women who were not compatible seemed more interested in the "idea" of Mark, rather than Mark as a fully realized person with wants and dreams. And Mark never invested in anyone emotionally, as who gets emotionally invested in his future android girlfriend?

She's supposed to be programmed to do the heavy emotional lifting, because aren't emotions a lady thing all ladies like to deal with? Why work that muscle when it was her job?

And such is the plight when we think of our significant others as artificial stereotypes instead of as real people.

Mark, with all his money and charm, couldn't hide the thing that turned ideal women off of him— his emotional distance. It's hard to get close to someone when you can't even tell if he's interested, if he's the same way with you as he is with a stranger on the street or a distant friend. For any relationship to work—male or female—you have to be vulnerable.

The right woman didn't care if Mark opened up his wallet. She wanted him to open up his heart.

But like a lot of men, Mark hadn't been raised to value his nurturing skills. Admitting your true nature—that you're not like everyone else—was a fear. If a woman knew all the soft and tender parts of him, she could hurt him. By being emotionally distant, he could control his search for the ultimate fembot.

Yet a relationship without vulnerability and emotion isn't a relationship at all. It's an agreement. And, after going around and around in circles over his wants versus needs, I finally got him to understand love wasn't going to "just happen" for him. He couldn't create a life and just plug any woman into it and expect it to be magical.

The same went for the women who pursued Mark because of his "traditional" male breadwinner attributes. In their pursuit of their "ideal," these women dressed, decorated and designed themselves to fit the type they thought a well-heeled, successful man would want.

Many of these women thought they knew the blueprint for success with the Marks of the world, as TV had told them time and time again: The only thing that matters is looking good.

Or, as I like to call it, the "reality TV effect."

Ever notice how on every reality show, no matter where the women come from or what they do, they all are starting to look alike? The piled-on studio makeup, layered and colored for maximum impact— even when they're going to bed for the night. The same boobs shaped like perfectly round globes shoved into the same form-fitting bandage dresses. The same high heels that look like hooves. The same super straight, super long hair. The same noses. The same voices. The same attitudes.

The look has made its way into our everyday lives. Women assume the Marks of the world want an arm piece, a pretty girl who doesn't think much or have all that much to say. And on the surface, it may seem that way, as Mark was unintentionally looking for a sympathetic android. But why didn't these plastic girls land the emotionally distant Mark?

Because these artifices they'd created were lies. You can't hide your true nature.

Your true nature isn't a stereotype.

Mark couldn't hide the contempt he felt in being with someone who only wanted him for what he could do for them. He couldn't relate to someone who didn't share his values or interests. And the various arm pieces couldn't hide who they were. Even though they were draped in the "reality" uniform, inside they were individuals with quirks, ambitions, tastes and values all their own, often running completely contrary to who Mark was and what he wanted. Looking like a fembot could get you in the door with Mark, but it couldn't get you past date number two if neither could find some commonality to bond over.

He was rich and she was hot . . . but now what?

Mark had to learn that he needed to emotionally invest so he could better get to know the women he was dating, so he could see what their true natures were and they could, in turn, see his. By revealing who he really was—a bright, big-hearted guy who valued loyalty and kindness—and opening up about his own past, dreams and interests. In being himself and not simply a stoic stereotype, he was better suited to apply the skills he'd learned in business to find himself a spouse, getting serious about getting to know the women he dated and opening up to the ones who shared his values.

When you're putting together your dating check-list, you need to outline what you need versus the gender stereotypes you think you want. The difference between wants and needs is based on having a clear understanding of which things impact your core health and happiness.

Things that don't impact this are wants.

Case in point: Mark wanted an athletic, pretty woman in her twenties who was fun, agreeable and wouldn't get jealous of his job or the many women he met at his restaurant.

What Mark "needed" was a woman who equaled him in confidence and was self-motivated, who saw herself as a whole person—not half a person waiting for Mark to make her whole. The fembots seemed to be ideal, because in the beginning they were always agreeable, but sooner or later, they would reveal themselves to be personally insecure. The reason why they had so much time to invest in Mark's interests and career was because they had no real ambitions or dreams of their own. Mark was supposed to be the *be all, end all* to their fairy tale, and they were often intimidated by his not "needing" them.

Mark needed an equal to be happy. She had to have her own life, and therefore would respect his career and goals, as she would expect him to respect her own.

Athletic is nice. Young is nice. But what if there was a gorgeous woman of thirty-four, with her own career, who shared Mark's disinterest in having children and respected his need to devote time to his business? Is she a "no-go" because she's too skinny or too tall, or too curvy or five years older than what he had in mind?

A stereotype isn't a prerequisite to happiness. When we see others as individuals, we view people the same way we would like others to view ourselves. We also make better dating decisions.

Are you seeing the people you date as individuals or as stock characters in a film called *My Life*? Ask yourself these questions:

1. If one friend has grown up with a father who cheated on his or her mother and another friend grew up with a father who was always faithful, does this mean the latter friend is an anomaly and/or lying?

2. Do you think marriage can't work unless it is a traditional marriage with well-defined gender roles?

3. A man wants to stay at home to raise his child—is he lazy, leeching off his wife's hard work?

4. Your partner doesn't want children—do you think it's because they're selfish or are simply saying so because it sounds "different"?

5. If your partner tells you they don't like

something that you care for or believe in, do you find yourself "testing" them to see if they're being truthful?

6. Do you expect your partner to cheat on you, treat you poorly or take advantage of you because "that's what they all do"?

7. If your partner does something you don't like or disagree with, do you believe you can get or force them to change?

It's important to remember that everyone's life story and experiences are valid. Challenge your own beliefs and judge people on their merits—not what you think or society thinks they should be doing. Make up your own mind based on their attitude and efforts—not gendered expectations.

CHAPTER 3

Love Yourself Before Someone Else

When I first met Jason he thought I was a pimp.

Handsome and successful, he was more than experienced at the dating game. A little too experienced in fact. He had a goal that began and ended with getting a girl to his (or her) bedroom and beyond that, not much else. He wasn't serious, except that he wanted me to do the hard work for him—finding new sexual conquests—freeing up more time so he could focus on his career.

But I had little interest in playing the role of sexual conquest headhunter or "hit it and quit it" wingman for hire.

Still, I wanted to work with Jason, if only to understand why he was so consumed with conquest, having little to no interest in relating to women as human beings.

Jason talked about clothes. He talked about his car. He talked about his money, and women were just another extension, another symbol of that success. He didn't want to be close to anyone and didn't see the point. The fun was in the hunt. Who wanted to invest in what happened post-coitus? Only a weaker man would desire comfort or romance over conquest, he thought. Being trapped by a woman's love and relying on them, needing them, seemed foolish.

Why want something that's impossible to have and will only bring you trouble if you get attached?

And that was the point when I realized something much darker was going on with Jason that went beyond a love of sex with different lovely ladies and "conquest." Jason was a wounded soul.

I agreed to help Jason if he was open to finding love, not just a lay, but Jason was resistant to love. Once we got past the stereotypes about "men never wanting to marry" or "men not having the ability to be faithful to one woman," Jason's desire to hit it then quit it was born out of deep hurt that he rarely examined.

His mother had committed suicide when he was five years old.

Jason's mother had struggled with mental illness

all her life and like many individuals suffering under the stigma of mental illness, she believed her son would be better off without her. She thought she was "damaged," and that her psychological pain would only be spread to her son. Young and not understanding why, Jason saw his mother's suicide as abandonment and betrayal. And these feelings of hurt were only exacerbated when his eldest sister, his long-time caretaker as a child, passed away from cancer.

When Jason loved a woman, she left him. And as he revealed to me the real reason why he was focused on conquest over commitment, it wasn't that Jason didn't desire it—in fact, he was desperate for it. But why get close to someone who was just going to leave anyway? Even if she loved you. She could just leave through suicide or illness. And the pain from the loss was too great to risk again with a girlfriend or wife. But he still desired the closeness, the satisfaction that he'd get from dating and having sex with a woman. It was a substitute for the affection lacking in his life, but now he couldn't separate emotional intimacy from sexual intimacy. The two were so wrapped around each other, mixed with his own disappointment and self-loathing, rooted in his mother's suicide.

I told Jason he didn't need a matchmaker. He needed a therapist.

It's hard to get on the path to love when you're at war with yourself.

The battlefield of love is filled with victims, saddled with the post-traumatic stress of previous interpersonal failings. They wander with wounded hearts, struggling to build long-lasting ties to others. They substitute sex for real intimacy. They trade materialism for trust. They carry with them the baggage of old slights and pains, pathologies and parental issues. They don't want to get hurt again, so they don't give anything up they believe they can't afford to lose.

And the main thing they can't afford to lose is their damaged heart.

But if your goal is love, you're never going to get it in a healthy way unless you finally get right with yourself. Building self-worth and confidence go a long way in making you happier and more attractive to those you desire. You're not going to get (or keep) the one you love with an attitude, aggression or constant belittling and disrespect. This means that for many men, you have to get in touch with your inner feminist and kick out your outer sexist. And for many women, if you can't trust, you can't love. And we all need to learn how to respect our significant other's space.

Finding inner peace can have great outer results—like lower stress levels, healthier relationships and having greater patience when life gets a little crazy. And we can find that peace in our personal lives, our friends, our families, our hobbies, our work and our faith. We can do good for ourselves and find the good within us that propels us along, to a better version of us.

While for some, the road to self-acceptance is paved with letting go of past fears and anxieties and embracing life with more vigor, for others—like Jason—a little outside help may be in order.

About one out of four Americans is annually afflicted with some mood disorder according to the National Institute of Mental Health. That's anything from depression to anxiety to bipolar disorder to post-traumatic stress disorder. Yet it's still taboo for many of us to speak out about these afflictions. Meaning there are a lot of emotionally wounded walking around, struggling to make connections. It also means there's a pretty good chance you or someone close to you might be one of them. Personal hurts are important to deal with, especially since they can indirectly affect your career, health and happiness. In relationships when we feel insecure or unhappy with ourselves, we may find that we look to our significant others to "fix" what we can only fix ourselves.

Again, how many Hollywood films have you watched where a damaged individual is transformed by love? A fairy tale where a man who was once an abusive, vicious beast turns into a handsome prince with the help of an understanding woman like *Beauty and the Beast*, or a sexist, racist jerk, like Jack Nicholson's character in *As Good As It Gets*, who's transformed by the love of the benevolent single mother character played by Helen Hunt. Never mind the entire book and film franchise of Stephenie Meyer's *Twilight*, where a teenage girl wins the love and compassion of a hundreds-year-old vampire who desires to love, control and (possibly) murder her.

There's no mental ailment that fiction says a little lovin' can't fix. But while there's an exception to every rule, many people who are abusive when single just continue to be abusive as part of a couple. Love can't cure what you can only fix yourself.

But you can, out of dysfunction, put that expectation on your significant other, then watch you both fall into destruction when a new boyfriend or girlfriend doesn't cure your hatred of the father who abandoned your family when you were twelve, or your crippling low self-esteem and body issues stemming from childhood bullying.

How can we find honest love when we haven't been honest with how we feel about ourselves? Past hurts can lead to some pretty destructive behaviors for those wanting healthy relationships.

Such as:

- Having an overall lack of trust—all actions are fraught with suspicion, no matter how benign

- Feeling pressure to change who you are to get love

- Unwillingness to compromise

- Manipulation and control issues

- Defining your worth by whether you have a romantic partner

- Being afraid to ever disagree with your partner

- Lack of privacy (like an insecure partner demanding to be with you always—even the examination room for routine doctors' appointments—or making you give them all the passcodes to your e-mail or social networking accounts)

- Neglecting yourself or your partner

- An unwillingness to be open or vulnerable emotionally in the relationship

- Feeling you have to stop doing things you enjoy to get love from your partner

- Always having to explain yourself and your actions, such as what you do, where you go and who you see

- Feeling forced or obligated to have sex or your partner insisting on unsafe sex

- Yelling or physical violence

Any of these behaviors are indicators that the real problem in your relationship is inside either yourself or your partner and your or their past pains. Unless that past pain is dealt with through self-reflection, therapy or, in some cases, mental health diagnosis and medication, it will linger or worsen.

No amount of love will ever fix what someone can only change themselves.

Self-change can come from many places. We can reach out for the support of friends and family or a medical expert. We can seek out mentors or spiritual guides. We can engage in our world in a new way, trying new activities, educating ourselves of things that take us outside of our present way of viewing the world. We can exercise body and mind. We can develop better coping mechanisms and work toward the actualization of self.

The important thing is to recognize the issue,

then take steps to deal with it. Instead of letting problems and slights linger as we suppress them, take care of your problems right away. Don't let them grow to a point where we feel they are too big to manage—and we're too ashamed to ask for help.

Other things you can do:

Check yourself: If you find your mind wandering into negative territory, stop and ask yourself where this is coming from, then refute the negative message with a counter message of self-worth. A friend of mine who suffered from depression and anxiety found that when she was down on herself she would read her résumé, reminding herself of what she had accomplished in her twenty-year career; she would read an old letter from her father, praising her artwork; or she'd look at an old photo tied to a good memory of a day she felt was successful—like her college graduation photo or a picture from a family vacation. It's good to have on hand evidence to refute the negativity in your mind.

Write it out: Keeping a journal, or taking inventory of the good things about your life, is a great way of reminding yourself that your world is bigger than whatever is bothering you today. It's also a great way to keep track of your moods and write out your problems—and their possible solutions.

Give yourself a break: When you find your mind wandering down a dark path, stop whatever you're doing and turn to an activity that is more rewarding, positive or—at least—distracting to you. Go exercise. Go for a walk. Clean. Eat a light snack if you're hungry. Listen to a favorite song or stretch out for a bit. Take a break to chat with a friend or do some light reading. Often a nice distraction will give you a break from what's troubling you so you can get back on track later.

Jason told himself he didn't want love because love was a trap. But he didn't want to touch on why he thought love was trap. It didn't occur to him that the pain that was inflicted on him from his mother's death was a pain he was taking out on the many women he dined, bedded and never saw again. Even when Jason told me he was willing to try dating healthily, once he confided in me his past hurts I realized he couldn't date or be open with a woman until he got help first.

Jason reluctantly agreed to see a therapist and after a few months I heard from him again. He admitted that he was making some healthy progress in better understanding himself and what happened to his mother and sister.

As he worked on himself, Jason took a break from dating, and I thought this was best. He needed to take himself out of the game until he was ready to approach dating in a healthy way that was fair to both himself and the women he desired. Through identifying his self-destructive, self-sabotaging behavior (in Jason's case this was being emotionally withholding and distant in a desire to not become attached to anyone), he gained much-needed self-awareness. Through that self-awareness he could take the steps he needed to refocus and then rejoin the dating game with a much more healthy approach. Namely one where he saw women as people—just like himself—who had their own ideas and goals and wants and past hurts.

And Jason wasn't my only client who struggled with internal issues. I've worked with women who seemed to only be attracted to abusive or emotionally damaged men because they tapped into their need to "rescue" or fix a broken man. I've worked with men who struggled with infidelity, not realizing that their need to pursue sex so doggedly was rooted in long-fermenting insecurities. I've worked with men and women who were bitter and untrusting due to broken hearts, broken families or their own broken psyches. Then there were the many people who simply weren't happy with themselves—those of us who feel we don't deserve love because we don't think we're good enough or pretty enough or don't make enough money and are battling internal demons, such as depression and severe mental illness. These individuals often sought love as a distraction to keep them from focusing on their own pain.

Unfortunately in putting all of their problems in the relationship basket, putting the burden of happiness on a person on the outside, rather than on what's going on internally, they were doomed to failure.

As the old saying goes, nobody can love you if you don't love yourself. Jason is dating healthily now and for the first time in years is open to really getting to know a woman in some way other than simply carnally. Jason also for the first time in years feels emotional peace about who he is and what happened with his mother and sister. He knows that while he will always miss them, he can't carry the burden of familial losses into his future relationships.

He can love and he can learn. And if you're dealing with past hurt, so can you.

Belgian Aussie musician Gotye sang, "You can get addicted to a certain kind of sadness" in his hit 2011 track "Somebody That I Used to Know"—so how's that working for you? Ask yourself, do you find any of these statements true?

1. When people leave you it is because they aren't strong enough.

2. Love is so hard to find that it could take years, even decades, to get over an ex. Especially if he or she was "the one."

3. When people don't agree with you or want you it is a rejection of who you are.

4. I think it's romantic to love someone even if they don't love me back. Even if the relationship isn't a good one, the fact that I was willing to go the distance shows I truly cared.

5. Human beings aren't capable of being faithful.

6. When people leave you it is because you are not worthy of their love.

7. Fighting is just part of a relationship. If my partner doesn't get mad or yell at me I start to wonder if they actually care.

If you found yourself agreeing with any of these statements, ask yourself why. What made you lose hope in your ability to find a healthy relationship?

CHAPTER 4

Know Your Relationship Vitals

Back in 2010, a popular, satirical YouTube video called "(Authentic) Black Marriage Negotiations" was tweeted and Facebooked and e-mailed around featuring a computer animation of a black woman listing all the things she wanted in a man.

While the clip was loathed by the many who pushed it toward having the more than six hundred thousand views it had at the time of my writing this book, the video tapped into what has been a big issue in my work: people being unable to tell values from wants.

As the computer animation rattled off her laundry list of things she desired in a mate, it reminded me that both men and women—regardless of race—

sometimes get a little too fixated on what "type" of mate they want rather than on a person who shares their values.

Among the cartoon's desires:

- A man who will pay all the bills yet recognize she is an independent woman

- An educated man

- A thug

- A man who can take charge, lead and direct his household, until she disagrees with his direction

- A man of God

- A baller, etc.

Most of the desires are contradictions to point out the absurdity of having any kind of list for anyone, and the video inspired many copycats and responses from a variety of perspectives.

And while that's all good for a laugh in the war of the sexes, that doesn't change the fact that quite a few men and women approach me with a laundry list of qualifiers as though shopping for a mate is like purchasing a car. You may be looking for a partner with low mileage, great miles-per-gallon, brand recognition and elite status—but there's no guarantee the Maybach of spouses is the right spouse for you.

Beauty and wealth. Education and class. They all sound good on paper, but you can meet the most beautiful, wealthy, educated aristocrat of your dreams and they could be an amoral beast. To get the love we want we have to learn how to move beyond types and look for love based on common values and complementary personality. Love doesn't come from "type hype."

What's "type hype"? Again, let's look to Hollywood, but this time to a film that's a bit more realistic in how "type hype" can doom a relationship—the hit 2009 Joseph Gordon-Levitt–starring romance, *(500) Days of Summer.* In it, Gordon-Levitt's character, a hopeless romantic, desires a quirky, lovey-dovey girl who will turn his life around, and he thinks he's found her in Zooey Deschanel's character, Summer. Summer is routinely described as being the "perfect" girl for Gordon-Levitt's character, Tom, despite the fact that Summer doesn't seem all that serious or interested in Tom. Tom regularly projects what he wants to see in Summer—which is a sort of stock film character known in movie lingo as the "Manic Pixie Dream Girl." This character is a woman with no real motivation of her own who exists solely to advance the story line of the main male character through her odd, precocious cuteness. She's basically a less princess-y version of Belle from Disney's *Beauty and the Beast,* dressed in hipster clothes, who collects odd knick-knacks and is fueled by "quirk." Tom ignores all obvious signs of potential failure—like the fact that she doesn't believe true love is possible and doesn't desire marriage—and simply homes in on how ideal her beauty is, how she's good at karaoke, how she dresses in an adorable fashion and says funny/quirky things.

When she finally ends the relationship and (spoiler alert) gets engaged to someone else, Tom is left flummoxed. She was his "type," his dream girl. How could the exact pretty, funny, weird girl he'd always desired be wrong for him?

Because Tom was caught up in the hype. (Which, to be honest, if you've seen the film, he never really gets over, as he ends the film projecting his lovey-dovey daydream on a new girl named Autumn.) Maybe if he kisses enough female oddballs he'll find the Lucille Ball to his Ricky Ricardo, but having a "type" is no indicator of relationship success because "type" has absolutely nothing to do with the most critical factor in whether your relationship will last—the values and personality of the person you are dating.

In creating a good match, you have to take stock of your "relationship vitals"—things that make up the core of what you want and believe in—then take stock of the things that are "non-starters," aka the things that would kill a potential relationship, like if your partner doesn't believe in monogamy and you do, or if you don't want kids, but your potential partner wants a basket-ball team. From there, take stock of your personality and the personality of your partner—are you both introverts? Extroverts? Are you more driven and is he more of a supporter? Do you mesh? And take stock of your level of physical attraction and how important that is to you to be sexually attracted to your partner.

I've found in my practice that if you can confirm that a partner shares your top values, has a personality that meshes well with your own, meets your non-starters, and there is a healthy level of romantic attraction, your chance of making a successful match goes from virtually nothing (about .04 percent) to a nearly 50 percent chance.

But in order to make that match you need to be able to:

1. Distinguish between a non-starter (need) and a preference (want).

2. Learn what your core personality type is.

3. Understand how your personality fits or is compatible with other personality types.

Early on in my matchmaking practice, I met Kyle. He claimed, at forty-two, he was ready to get serious about settling down, but he had some "expectations" of what he wanted in a woman, and those expectations were pretty rigid. She had to be under thirty-five, without kids, a non-drinker/smoker (not even socially), physically fit and a vegan. Ultimately, Kyle wanted someone to have children with (being a man and unable to produce progeny without a little help from a woman), and that was pushing his sudden desire to settle down.

But he had no interest in settling for anything less than what he wanted.

And Kyle found her a year after he met with me. She fit nearly everything on his checklist and they married quickly, only there was one hitch. When it came time to have kids, they couldn't conceive. But it wasn't the fault of his near perfect bride.

Kyle was impotent.

As important as it was for her to be vegan, to be in shape and to be alcohol- and tobacco-free, the only thing Kyle really wanted was a family. That was always the priority and the reason behind his push to settle down. But in the end, those things didn't hold as much value to him as the ability to have kids.

And, in his mind, his failure at that was his own fault.

Kyle had sought a wife to have his children, but not a wife who actually complemented his personality or met any of his emotional needs. Without a child, she was a hollow victory—a "perfect" girl he didn't have all that much in common with other than she is what he thought he wanted. She wasn't particularly understanding or empathetic when she realized he couldn't give her children. She didn't share any of his personal interests—political or regarding his career. There was that spark, but what would sustain it now that the impetus for marrying was gone? Both were facing the prospect of a lifetime—without kids—with a partner who is all type and shares none of their values.

Although Kyle's inability to have children wouldn't have changed no matter who he married, because he viewed his potential spouse as a series of checks on a list, he'd ignored the most important factor—whether they were actually compatible.

After the initial rush and passion of a new romance, after the sex, after time passes, you will eventually get used to your partner. You will get older. Your needs or desires may change with time. And at some point, all the great sex and good looks in the world won't cover for the fact that if you can't get along with your partner, if you don't enjoy spending time with them or talking to them, if you aren't friends—it's not going to work.

It's like the befuddlement one feels when someone cheats on a gorgeous actor or actress. People lament, how could he or she run out on one of the most beautiful people in the world?

Because beautiful doesn't equal "we'll get along."

Beautiful doesn't equal happiness.

Beautiful doesn't mean they're a good person or stable person or kind person or the right person for you.

Beautiful is just that. Beautiful. A gorgeous person could be faithful or they could be a cheat, but their looks are no real indicator for what truths lay in their personality. A beautiful person can be insecure, they can be shallow, they can be mean or emotionally ugly. Because "beautiful" is a "type," not a value.

Values are the things that tell you who is right for you.

And who is right for you?

If you're ready to throw your list away that says your dream man must be 6'1", have dreadlocks, an advanced degree from a prestigious university, White House connections and the skin tone of a young Denzel Washington in *Mo' Better Blues* and get to what kind of man (or woman) is actually right for you, you need to figure out who you are.

Figuring out what your values are is as simple as asking yourself: "What do I want out of life?"

And you don't need to list out elaborate details. If your goal is to have a successful business or to attain financial stability, reduce it to one- or two-word descriptions, such as "successful" and "financially stable."

These are your values. As you think about what you want in your own life, what contentment and stability and happiness look like to you, jot down about ten or fifteen items. When you're done, you have what you value most.

The list might look a bit like this:

Love

Family

Financial security

Success

Spirituality

Contentment

Consistency

Excitement

Home ownership

Travel

From there, prioritize your list of what means the most to you down to what is nice but not a deal breaker. For instance, perhaps you'll feel like a failure if you never have children, but never owning a home wouldn't make your life feel like a complete waste of existence.

Then determine what your personality type is and

how you can mix and match and complement other personality types to get you what you value in a relationship—not just what's pleasing to you in theory.

There are four main personality types based on the research of psychologist Carl Jung: analyst, controller, supporter and promoter.

The analyzer is primarily concerned with being right. This leads to their constantly researching, testing and gathering copious amounts of information before making a decision. They're big on weighing options. Analyzers are conscientious and often think through how their actions will affect others and tend to be fairly objective in their views. They're also pretty big on rules and maintaining standards.

The controller is all about the end game. In fact, they probably have used the phrase "the ends justify the means" several times in their lives because they are so task- and results-oriented. They're self-starters, can be somewhat rigid and make decisions quickly, but they also don't always listen very closely to the needs and opinions of others. After all, if you're a controller, you already believe you know which is the right way to go.

The supporter is a loyal individual, dedicated and committed to whatever they do. They are group-identified, meaning they prefer to be part of a duo or team. They are often extremely patient, understanding and are good listeners. Highly dependable, supporters are good at reaching a point of consensus with others—meaning they're good negotiators. Supporters often exhibit "beta" personality types. They're good partners or worker bees.

The promoter is high-energy and a lot of fun—but not very disciplined. They're very creative, charming, often take the lead in relationships, are motivators, competitive and "big picture" people. Details are just little things they'd rather not think about as they work on their master plans. Highly social, promoters seek lots of feedback from others, and are natural risk takers.

If you're a high-energy, super charming promoter, you might think it would sound like electrifying fun to date, or even marry, your fellow social butterfly, however, we typically match up better with those who have the personality traits we're lacking and need some balance for.

For example, a friend of mine, Celena, is an outgoing extroverted "promoter" type. She's a lot of fun, full of ideas and highly charismatic. But she's also very undisciplined and unfocused. Her longtime partner, Jake, is an introverted, dependable and quiet supporter type. He's as reliable as the sun shining, an only child, and at certain times of his life has been a loner. But just because Celena liked being high-energy didn't mean she wanted to run around on "10" all the time. And just because Jake liked being alone to focus on his artwork and reading, that didn't mean he didn't want to go out and try new things.

Perfect match.

Celena got Jake to get out more and take more risks. With her motivation skills and love of social settings, she was happy to help Jake navigate the world of fine-art networking to help him get his paintings out of his bedroom and into a gallery. For Celena, Jake got her to calm down and take the time to think out her problems rather than just react emotionally. His being centered helped her stay centered, reducing her anxiety greatly. Plus, she needed someone who could be there for her during rough patches in her emotional life, as Celena often vacillated between extreme highs and lows and needed someone stable like Jake to keep her feet planted firmly in reality.

Celena had dated other promoters before. They were a whirl of passion and energy and then, finally, nothingness. They would float up so high they would eventually float away from each other.

And Jake had dated other supporters. Which meant he never really left his house very often to do anything and he was stuck at a job he didn't like, living in a city he didn't care for. He wanted to change but wasn't sure how. But when he was with other supporters, change was the last thing on their minds—especially when they were waiting on beta-male Jake to initiate it.

Jake was the engine and Celena was the starter. Together, they kept each other going.

If Jake had said his "dream woman" was a type unrelated to his personality needs, Jake would probably say he liked a tall, athletic woman of high intellect, who doesn't drink alcohol or eat meat, with a hot curvy body, an adventurous sexual nature and little emotional complications. And before Celena, he did date a lot of these women—they tended to be models or on television or they were aspiring models and/or TV personalities. While they most certainly were hot, sexually viable and even smart, many of them also turned out to be personally dull, shallow, mean or not supportive of Jake. They all thought Jake was hot since he was so tall, dark and handsome, but they didn't like that he was such a homebody, they didn't like his goofy sense of humor, they didn't like the fact that he was a broke artist, they didn't like that he didn't care about celebrity or fashion or impressing others. Jake had zero interest in social climbing or crass materialism. Jake was a "nice" guy, but "nice" didn't meet their needs.

If Celena had been asked about who her type was, she would have wanted an eyeglasses-wearing genius. Some brilliantly creative, charming type who wasn't too handsome but wasn't too ugly. Tall but not too tall. Preferably with an advanced degree working in some high-powered, influential profession. And she had dated some of those guys, and many of them had turned out to be boring, emotionally distant, controlling, focused on their career or schooling to the exclusion of everything else, mean-spirited or neurotic. Celena was the charming nerd girl they thought they wanted, until they realized her high energy and high emotions were unwanted distractions.

Jake's no professional, but he meets Celena's core values. And he balances her out. Celena, while very cute, is no fashion model, but she has the right balance of fun and ambition Jake needed to get out of his career rut.

While we might be tempted to date what we see in the mirror, what we really need is a nice contrast. It's not quite opposites attract (as Jake and Celena share core values of intellect, stability, fidelity and loyalty), but that variety complements. A man or woman obsessed with a checklist does him- or herself in by excluding their true personality and needs. Celena thought she always wanted to be with some intellectual titan, not the homebody goofball Jake can be from time to time, and Jake thought looks trumped all, but when smart doesn't mean you understand emotion and looks don't always mean you're fun to spend time with, it's better to focus on your shared values.

Type hype can't sustain a love, but a good balance can.

Ditch the checklist and find out what really matters to you.

Make a list of what your relationship vitals are:

Values are tangible things related to conditions, personality or a code of beliefs/personal ethics (i.e., "likes children," "stable," "adventurous," "good humored"), not wants (i.e., "must be over six feet tall," "must be a size six," "must be a Republican").

Rank your relationship values in order of importance:

Identify your personality based on the four types listed (analyst, supporter, controller, promoter).

Make a list of your relationship non-starters:

_____

_____

_____

CHAPTER 5

Get Over the Word "No"

Do you like me? Check "yes" or "no."

It's amazing how what once seemed so earth-shattering to us as children can still bind us as adults. The immediacy of youth gave way to the gravity of adulthood, and yet we're still wounded creatures of habit and feelings. Rejection hurts, and we learn that at an early age.

Back when we thought the world began and ended with us, our wants, needs and desires, the word "no" was simply another tool in the arsenal of getting our way. The two-year-old child inside of us relished in our ability to scream to the heavens the magic word that was supposed to end the things we did not like and destroy the things we despised. And "no" is always fine if you're the one who gets to deliver it, if you're the one who gets to determine the behavior, if you get to set the rules of what is acceptable and what is not.

But if the pint-size, junior version of you felt empowered to say to the world "no," so did we all. And while "no" was a declaration of your independence, hearing someone say "no" was a declaration of your irrelevance. Hearing "no" was being told you were wrong, that you do not have control; it's a rejection. And it stings.

In the world of dating and mating, there is a type of person for whom "no" is just another word, and chances are, you have met him. He approaches the field of romance as a game where anyone and everyone is potentially a player. He pursues love by the volume, shouting out intentions from bus stops and bar counters, dance floors and church pews. He's in the supermarket aisles, preying on smiles, shouting come-hither lines on any and everyone who seems in play. Heck, even if you're not in play. A woman on her own is fair game in his mind.

Most of the time he's rejected. Women are typically pretty disgusted by him. He's not very sophisticated or even smart. But he has something most of us do not possess—he no longer fears the word "no." He has discovered that if you hit on ten different girls, no matter how off-putting or odd your come-ons, at least one girl will say "yes." It's a numbers game, and in the end, he wins it—if only because he'll never stop asking. Things like a person being better-looking, wealthier, smarter, better dressed, better connected mean nothing to him. Because it's about the volume. The more you ask, the better the shot. The more opportunities, the more the odds go in your favor.

"No" is just another way of saying, "Ask someone else."

While you may recoil in horror for the man lacking in any kind of discrimination or taste, while you may find him repulsive, in his own way, he has already beat you. Because he is fearless, he can bank on you not being fearless. Your fear means someone out there will be willing to "settle" for him because that someone never knew you were an option.

And so many women complain that no nice guys ever approach them. And so many men lament that they can't meet the right girl. And how often has it been because our fear of "no," our low self-esteem, our insecurities, kept us out of the game. Yet being out of the game is why when you see that nice guy with that horrible girl, or that nice girl with that terrible guy, you start singing, "Is she really going out with him? Is she going to take him home tonight?" You created an environment where the dating scavenger who asks women out by volume can survive.

Your fear of "no" has made you part of the problem when it's time to be the solution.

Instead of being disgusted by Mr. Asks-Out-By-Volume, take a cue from him—don't be afraid of the word "no."

Would you have the job you have if you hadn't applied for it? Would you have attended the college you wanted if you had not prepared, studied, passed those classes, gotten your high school diploma, taken the SAT or ACT and applied? Would you be in the house, apartment, city, state you wanted to be in if you hadn't taken some initiative? Somehow, at some point, you got over the word "no" when it came to your education, career or place of residence.

So why are you still so afraid of the attractive stranger in your midst?

When you're proactive, you are rewarded. Just as it is in your education or career, dating is no different. To win, you have to play. Sit on the sidelines and you'll get sidelined results. Maybe, just maybe, the coach will notice how you've so quietly and diligently worked away, never said a word, and suddenly, apropos of nothing, put you in the game and you'll dunk on the first dribble out, but . . . let's be real.

That's not how it goes.

You work, you hustle, you vie for the coach's attention. You beg, cajole, threaten, lobby, hustle your way into getting in that game and then you make the most of those few moments in an effort to prove your worthiness. And whether you succeed or fail in that first court outing, your goal is always to get back out there and stay out there as long as possible until success comes to you.

Yet in dating, what do we do? We expect it to "just happen." We expect it to be easy. We don't plan. We don't hustle. We don't study. We expect a Disney cartoon of "happily ever after" and fireworks. Not real work. Not getting outside our heads and outside of ourselves and doing the heavy lifting.

Especially if you're a beta male or female.

Everyone is familiar with the pop psychology of alpha personality types. They're outgoing, confident, not afraid of "no." They have the charm and social skills you only get from being fearless at the trial and error it takes to master social interactions. They're considered to be aggressive, go-getters, ambitious, even arrogant. Betas, or "type B" personality types are supposed to be more of the go-along-to-get-along-gang of personas. They work well in groups, are good consensus builders, are thoughtful and cautious. But all that good stuff about community building and supportive tendencies gets lost in the one thing beta personality types are considered not to be—proactive.

Alphas make things happen. Betas have things happen to them. You may be an alpha in your career or education, but due to long-standing fears of rejection stemming from your childhood, you may be a beta when it comes to romance.

Let's be real here—rejection hurts. I'm not telling you your pain and acrimony aren't real. But I am saying that the weight you put on those hurt feelings is possibly out of proportion of the totality of your experience. What do you really lose when you go after what you want? You see a gorgeous man or woman you desire and you approach them and they say no. What did you really lose? They were never yours to possess to begin with. The only thing you have impacted is your pride.

Is your pride so important that it should achieve prominence over your personal happiness?

Which brings us back to our example of the man who asks women out by volume.

Author Neil Strauss chronicled his rise from average, frustrated casual dater to "guru-level" pickup artist in his book *The Game*, which highlighted the underground world of the pickup artist game, a cabal of men teaching other men manipulative techniques to tip the odds in their favor in the dating game.

While Strauss and the cohorts he made focused on techniques to move them from the sidelines to the bedroom of women they saw on the street, in bars and in clubs, there is one unifying factor in his advice that is applicable to us all—whether we're engaging in sexual conquest or looking for the loves of our lives: getting over rejection means getting serious about what we want.

Strauss and other pickup artists (or PUAs) put heavy emphasis on dedicating themselves to the craft of attracting women. That means taking a real-time assessment of who you are and how you look, then working to get yourself to a point where you are as attractive to who you desire as possible. They've long abandoned the "it'll just happen when it happens" mythology and actually applied themselves to the work of making themselves attractive to others.

While there are many unsavory aspects of PUAs—from some of the more controversial and manipulative techniques, such as playing on someone's insecurities to force a more positive outcome in your sexual favor—the core of getting over your fears and getting into the game is true for anyone who desires companionship. At some point, you have to get serious—especially about boosting your own confidence to tackle dating.

At the core of PUA techniques is building self-confidence, which means no more apologies for having desires, wanting love or existing. If you read as insecure when dating, you'll get treated as such. So to paraphrase these ego-boosters, remember:

- **No more excuses**—You deserve love and companionship regardless of your past experiences.

- **You have value**—Stop apologizing for existing. It's not all about them. You have just as much to offer in a relationship, so keep that in mind. It's not just about what greatness they could bring to your life, but that you bring your own greatness that they can benefit from as well.

- **The one you want doesn't want you? So what?**—You lose nothing when you never had the person to begin with. Knowing where you romantically stand with someone you desire is the path to eventually gaining romantic success. You learn from that initial rejection what works for you and what doesn't, who you want and who you don't want. Don't be so dependent on someone else's approval.

Self-confidence is what wins in the end in the game of attraction.

- **"No" is just another word for "try something else"**—So what? You got turned down. You weren't dressed right. You blurted something embarrassing. You revealed too much personal detail in an initial encounter. No one does everything right the first time. Learn from your experiences; evolve from your initial setbacks. Trial and error is the only way to get you into dating shape.

- **The word "no" doesn't control you**—Rejection only hurts for a little while. The more you get out there and interact, the less and less "no" matters. You'll find, in all actuality, that once you take the pressure off of expectation and the validation of strangers, meeting new people and getting to know them is fun. It's an adventure. Who will you meet this time? How will you get along? What will happen? Embrace the unknown. Instead of it making you want to give up, let "no" empower you. Let it challenge you.

- **You deserve love**—No matter how bad you think you are, remember there are people out there who don't think like you. You would probably say they have less than you—less to offer, less in personality, less in looks—yet nothing stops them. They go for what they want. Stop worrying about how you need to lose twenty pounds of fat or gain twenty pounds of muscle. Stop worrying about whether you have the right job, education or look. Make you the best you who you can be and consign yourself to the belief that you deserve love—not love if you were just a little different, but love as you are.

In all these modified mantras from the PUA handbook the core message is confidence. Confidence can take you further than a fancy car or a "hot" body. Your attitude and how you carry yourself will be the determining factors—who you are fundamentally is the determining factor of your romantic success.

And this isn't just about men; women need to get over "no" as well. This isn't Victorian England. We're no longer living in hunter-gatherer societies where biological imperatives determine that men will be the pursuer while women choose passively. Nothing is holding you back from approaching the man you want but your own wounded ego and hundreds of years' worth of social conditioning that has told you the man has to ask first—whether you want him to or not.

There's this prevailing thought that men, somehow, aren't effected by the word "no," when in fact many men fear it just as much as women. Only a special subset of men, such as our Mr. Asks-Out-By-Volume, has gotten over that fear. Many nice, well-meaning men who are potentially good partners never got over that initial insecurity and have channeled all their extroversion into their education or careers. They are equally reluctant to put themselves out there. Yet women have no more to lose in making the first move than men do—it's just a no. You don't die. You aren't banished to the land of the undateable. No one takes your relationship potential card. Nothing happens at all but those initial moments of rejection, passed over until the next interesting fellow comes along.

Over the past year and a half I have challenged my female clients to stop being passive and approach dating with the same vigor and fearlessness of a PUA. And this isn't about leaning out of a car and shouting things (that's just rude); this is simply about being the best of yourself and approaching those you desire with confidence. Online dating sites, from OkCupid to PerfectMatch.com, have revealed that for a woman to have a positive experience on their site, she needs to initiate contact. Why? Because there will always be that small percentage of guys who ask everyone out no matter their own personal skills or attractiveness. These men dominate the online space, as they know that if they send spam messages to over fifty or a hundred women online, about 5 to 10 percent of those women may turn into dates. But as a woman online, you have to go after what you want.

Unless you're happy with Mr. Asks-Out-By-Volume?

We can't be passive in love. Not if we want results.

In my summer dating challenge I proposed that women make a goal for themselves to go out on ten dates in one month. And you don't get those dates by sitting around waiting for the phone to ring. I encouraged women to ask out men until they met their ten quota. That meant going out, doing different things, getting outside of their comfort zone and getting used to talking to different kinds of men and being proactive instead of reactive.

This challenge is great for women in a dating rut or drought—meaning they never go on dates, are rarely asked out and don't introduce themselves to new situations with much regularity. The challenge

is largely the same for men who also deem themselves too shy to pursue women. It's about building
up that toughness you're lacking and getting over
that "no." You don't get the degree, make the free
throw or learn how to do the electric slide without
practice.

Dating is no different.

And if you're trying to attract others to you—
regardless of gender—my advice is as follows:

- **Be confident.** It's the main thing you
  need to do to get the best results.
  There is nothing more attractive than
  someone who feels good about who
  they are and knows what they want
  in life.

- **Look your best.** This isn't about
  changing who you are but accentuat-
  ing what you have. This means having great hygiene and styling and
  fashion that flatter your look and
  personality.

- **Smile.** How's anyone ever going to
  know you're available if you're scowl-
  ing at them?

- **K.I.S.S.—Keep it simple, sweetheart.**
  You don't need a gimmick. You just

need to be the best version of you. Avoid cheesy pickup lines and come-ons. Relax and let youself shine through.

- **Be memorable.** No one ever got what they wanted by being like everyone else. Find what's unique about you and accentuate it. Instead of playing down that thing that makes you different, play it up, embrace it and make it your signature.

- **Muffle your chatterbox.** If you don't listen, you miss out on all the important cues that let you know what's working for you and what's not. Before you open your heart you have to open those ears.

Somewhere there is a guy out looking for you. He's wondering where you are and why it's never you—charming, interesting, funny you—who approaches him. Stop missing out on this person and get yourself in the game.

You can't win the dating game if you never play.

I know it sounds scary, but it doesn't have to be; you just need to make a plan. Consider these plans of action as you prepare to get out and find some potentials:

1. Join a free online dating service or sign up for a trial period of a paid one.

2. Sign up for an activity you normally wouldn't engage in—like nature rides, an art appreciation class, Bible study, an amateur sports–related meet-up like a local kickball league or volunteer work.

3. Break away from who you know and find out who *they* know—meaning: networking!

4. Research your area's social calendar for mingling opportunities—from Chinese New Year to Cherry Blossom Festivals to the Taste of Chicago—get out and go where the people are!

5. Plan a day trip! Sometimes the best way to meet someone is to . . . get out and meet someone by going to an unfamiliar place you've always been curious to visit. Tour wine country or Civil War–era battlefields. Attend a music or pop art–based convention. Attend a trade show. Visit a neighboring city and explore new venues, bars and restaurants.

6. When you get a business card, phone number or message online—follow up! Don't let a contact languish. Even if you meet for coffee and find out they're not right for you, you never know who they may know.

7. Don't be afraid to make friends—not everyone is going to be your lover, but the more friends you have, the more people you know, the more chances you get to meet someone who may work for you.

8. Schedule those dates! Once you have piqued someone's interest in person or online and followed up with a prelimi-

nary chat online or over the phone, schedule a thirty-minute date for coffee and a conversation.

Don't be afraid to get out there and take some risks! The search for love is an adventure—embrace it!

CHAPTER 6

Sloppy Comes in Second

When I was a child I was a terrible speller but a decent writer, and for many of my teachers that was enough. They enjoyed my prose so much they gave me a pass on misspellings and grammatical errors and other flaws, and my father would pull me aside to tell me that I needed to clean up my act.

"Your writing speaks for you when you can't," he would say.

I can't say that I listened. But when I received my first-ever D in English 101 for turning in a series of comma splices and run-on sentences I called a term paper, I got it.

Sure, I was bright. But who would ever know that from what I wrote?

The same goes for who you are. The same goes for your dating profile.

If it looks sloppy, you get sloppy results.

How you dress on that first date. How you speak. How you behave. Your hygiene, your manners, your online dating profile, your reputation all speak volumes before the first words of flirtation come tumbling from your lips. If you want A-quality dates, you can't show up with your D-minus game.

A-level quality deserves an A-level effort.

But my mother likes me just how I am, you say. Great. I didn't know you were planning on dating your mother. But if you're going to jump in the shark-filled waters of the dating pool, you need to let go of your *Sesame Street* lessons of "it doesn't matter" and into the world of "oh, yes, my friend, it does."

It's not about changing you but being the best version of you.

First off, your mother lied to you: looks matter. Naturally, years of life experience have already taught you this, so I'm not necessarily shattering your worldview. And there's a science to beauty—having a symmetrical face, clear skin, looking healthy, having a "youthful" appearance as a woman and slightly "mature" appearance as a man—that will play heavily in your favor. And when it comes to weight and fitness, many factors come into play. Women statistically seem to prefer men who look slightly older than them, are taller and somewhat larger in weight or musculature. Men tend to prefer women who have a low waist-to-hip ratio, as rapper Sir Mix-A-Lot quite famously wrote a song about when he admitted to liking "big butts" and getting sprung "when a girl walks in with an itty-bitty waist."

Crude as that may be . . . *it's not really that far off.* With women, weight isn't so much of an issue as many think it is. It's all about proportions, and if people can see your silhouette, that "Coke bottle" body glorified in many classic beauties from Marilyn Monroe to Beyoncé, the poundage doesn't quite matter as much. And there's even an evolutionary reason for this, as women with pear-shaped figures—i.e., having larger hips and buttocks compared to their upper torso—have statistically fewer health problems than apple- or rounder-shaped women. Women with larger hips and a smaller waist have lower instances of heart disease, diabetes and other ailments; they're seen as more fertile and often have fewer problems in childbirth.

So Sir Mix-A-Lot's passion isn't so much of a fetish but part of our biological drive, even through our most frail fashion-model fads.

Slim fashion icon Twiggy still had a .70 waist-to-hip ratio.

All this goes back to the fact that looking good doesn't mean you have to look like a high-end fashion model or actor Ryan Gosling to find love. This just means you, again, need to look like the best version of you. If you have poor dental hygiene, see a dentist. If you have damaged skin—whether from acne scarring or sun damage—see a dermatologist and develop a skin-care regimen. Clip your fingernails and toenails. Bathe regularly. Invest in lotion to avoid dry skin. Floss your teeth. Wash, style and groom your hair with some consistency. Trim, shave, grow out or remove your facial hair in a way that best flatters you. Experiment with makeup. Get enough water, sleep and healthy foods. Make sure you're getting your daily allowance of vitamins. Exercise three times a week. Wear clothes that are clean and flattering to your physical look and personality.

Those are the looks that matter. That was especially the case for Andrew, one of my clients.

Andrew was a "cave man." He was only twenty-six, never married and in college. He was 5'10" and of average weight, but his physical appearance was sloppy and unkempt. And while that was fine for his career as a computer programmer, it didn't do much for his dating game, where he turned off or intimidated most women with his wild hair and beard and clothing choices that were more afterthought than fashion statement.

It wasn't that Andrew didn't have his charms. He was a great guy, nice, even-tempered, reliable, faithful and supportive. There was nothing he wouldn't do to help a family member, friend or stranger. He was a gentleman. But instead of women being drawn to his fidelity and kindness, they couldn't get past the fact that he didn't trim his fingernails with any regularity and that his teeth were stained from one too many caramel macchiatos.

But once Andrew realized his imposing look was really the only thing holding him back, he found success. He was already extremely smart, creative and funny. He just needed a little TLC. He didn't realize that no one is immune from playing the game of attractiveness. Both men and women make split-second decisions on whether to pursue or ignore based on simple attractiveness. But, again, this isn't about looking like actor Idris Elba. It's about not looking like the Unabomber.

We typically make our judgments on physical attraction within two hundred milliseconds. This means you can be sitting across from a great potential partner and not even notice it because their bad breath or filthy fingernails knock them right out of the game.

Helping clients who are just a little scruffy is actually a lot easier than most other cases. They usually already have strong work ethics and healthy personalities. Now it's just about presenting that in the best physical light. Andrew adapted quickly with a little help, not so much different from a piece of real estate that just needed some investment in its "curb appeal." Once his look was locked, his inner personality was magnified tenfold. His confidence followed, increasing with the ever-positive response he received from his much more approachable look, and now Andrew is currently engaged to be married.

Now back to how there are things that speak for you when you can't speak for yourself—namely, your clothes.

Some of this might seem like a no-brainer, but in our rush for comfort, we sometimes let our personal style slide. After all, we work hard jobs. We have family constraints and personal issues and it takes some effort to look nice. But if you're looking for love, you can't really afford to walk around with a heart saying you're open but a pair of pants saying you're anything but.

What do your clothes say about you?

Well, if you're sloppy—meaning, you seem to not care if you are wrinkled or mismatched or stained or out-of-style or raggedy—people will assume you, the human being, are a slob who doesn't care. People interpret "not caring" as "not available." And that's not caring and not available for everything—from dating to your career.

If you're decked out in designer duds, demonstrating how "put-together" you are, the flash might work for you for a bit, but it might also signal that you're unhealthily fixated on material gains, superficial or desperate to fit in. A high-end wardrobe doesn't always reveal a high-end persona. Sometimes you can appear to be overcompensating.

If you're an "extremist" dresser—as in, someone who wears outlandish things that could be mistaken for some kind of costuming—people may assume you are desperate for attention and overcompensating in an off-putting way. Unless your goal is to attract fellow extremists who dabble in your flavor of fashion shock—e.g., Goth enthusiasts, club kids, bikers or day vampires.

If you can't be bothered to cover up—e.g., your best outfit is the one that bares the most leg, neck, back or cleavage—you're sending quite an aggressive signal as well. Especially if you're scantily clad for non–night club environments like a company picnic or church. Too tight, too short, too low-cut clothing on men and women signals a desperation for attention that feeds into a perception that you are desperate for attention. And desperation is the last impression you want to give in a dating environment that favors the confident. While it's OK to sex it up from time to time, if your only shirt is a muscle shirt and your only pants are "hot" pants, you'll get the muscle shirt/hot pants, "he/she is not serious" treatment.

If you're "jeans 'n' T-shirt" all the time or always in your athletic gear, if you aren't mindful, you can get confused for being in the sloppy territory . . . or worse, you could appear drab and thoughtless in your fashion choices. People will assume you don't want to be bothered as you dressed in the most careless way possible.

And if you're the king or queen of business casual, if it's done with care and taste, you can project that air of confidence and security and responsibility you want others to see.

But these aren't hard and fast rules. You can find a healthy mix of the professionalism of business casual, with a bit of flirt appeal. You can take your sloppiness and push it through a hipster prism, creating a fetching outfit of delicious irony. You can add a bit of flash to your more conservative fashion choices that help you stand out—like an interesting pair of shoes or a funky handbag.

The best thing you can do is take how fashionable you are and either pump it up or straighten it out if it's too close to drab or sloppy, or tone it down or casual it up if you're too close to the too sexy, extreme or costumelike end of fashion.

But no matter what you wear:

- Wear clothes that fit.

- Wear clothes that flatter.

- Dress appropriately for the situation.

- Don't stress out over expense or label names—you make the clothes, the clothes shouldn't make you.

- Don't fret too much over trends.

- Try to always put some thought into what you wear—even to the gym or grocery store.

- Don't wear things that make you feel sloppy or unattractive.

- Be willing to take the occasional fashion risk and see how it fares.

- Wear what makes you feel comfortable and good.

- Show a little personality and have fun.

Now, after you've gotten all cleaned up, put on your best duds and plaster on a smile—take a picture. You're going to need it for your online profile.

OkCupid, an online dating site, has some of the best data-mining around about online profiles, namely your profile picture. And if you want to have a successful photo, men and women need to keep different things in mind.

Your Face

Women—You need to smile and look directly at the camera. Looking directly is a way of adding a level of personalization men pick up on. It also doesn't hurt to flirt with the camera a little, as long as you don't overdo it with tragic things like "duck lips" (that thing when you press your lips together to make a lazy sort of kissy face). But the key is smiling and making eye contact. If you're going to appear to be smiling at anyone, it should be at the person eyeballing your photo.

Men—You almost need to do the opposite. Smiling is a bit of a crapshoot when it comes to effectiveness, and you actually do better if you look away from the camera. As for camera-flirting, only do it with serious caution. For every man who can pull off "the people's flirty eyebrow" of former wrestler Dwayne "The Rock" Johnson, there are a lot of guys who just look goofy to their intended.

Your Body Position

Women—A little three-quarter shot never hurts. In fact, the little bit more your future paramours can see the better. This usually means taking a shot of yourself from a slightly overhead angle, contorting to fit more of your neck, arms and chest into a shot.

Men—Keep your shirt on. You're frightening everyone. (Unless your abs are, in fact, your best feature and you're under thirty.) Women tend to respond negatively to male photos that seem overly suggestive or overt. This is probably why eye contact works for women (men are used to women being passive and not making eye contact) and not for men (men making eye contact if it's unwanted are often perceived as threatening by women). But there are exceptions to every rule, namely if you have an enviable six-pack. Why hide your best assets? Although, if you want to be taken seriously, there may be more subtle ways to show off your body without looking like a show-off—such as action shots or clothes that fit properly. But avoid the outdoorsman/world travel photo—every guy has tried that one already.

Your Fashion Choices

For both men and women—keep it simple. For a man, getting too dressed up is a bit off-putting, but being casual is inviting. For women, a little cleavage doesn't hurt, but being too sexy in your fashion choices will play against you as you get older, much like Mr. No Shirt. You're simply not taken as seriously as you'd like—although when it comes to just getting attention, older women are penalized for cleavage as much as men are for shirtlessness.

Your Action Shot

For men and women—Do. Something. Interesting. Your profile shot is an insight into who you are—do you play music, are you an artist, do you write, do you work with computers, do you swim? A photo that creatively reflects your interests and tastes is a great conversation starter. It will especially help you stand out from the sea of bland bathroom camera-phone headshots that populate these online spaces.

And in all that with your online profile, always make sure it's updated, and keep it detailed but short. Humor is great, creativity is great, being fun and/or flirty without being too over-the-top is attractive. No matter what you do, you have to accentuate what the best part of you is. If you're a great writer, write a kick-ass profile. If you're a great artist, use one of your paintings for the profile photo.

And that's really what goes for everything. From your dress to your hair to your manners to your dating profile—it's about making you the best you, enhancing you and embracing what makes you special, fun, attractive and interesting. It's about putting that best face forward to entice would-be dates into wanting to get to know more about you.

It's about taking what's awesome about you and cranking up the volume, removing the static and polishing the sound production. It's about taking you from a ragtag production to professionalism.

All while still being wonderful, imperfect you.

Go to your closet and take a gander and let's take a stock of what we find . . . and what that means.

All your casual clothes are jeans and all your dress clothes are work suits.

> You play it safe and prefer to make clothes an afterthought. If life came with a uniform you just might wear it because you don't feel like you should have to spend your time worrying about what's on your back.

You're a woman and you don't own a pair of pants. Everything is a dress. Everything is a skirt.

> Well, this one depends on the length. If there's a variety of lengths, you're probably very feminine but also stylish. If they're all short, you must really be proud of your legs. And if they're all long, someone might mistake you for a very devout and conservative woman of faith. Or their grandmother.

You're a man who owns several throwback sports jerseys, T-shirts with cartoon characters on them and jeans, but you've never bought a suit . . . let alone a suit jacket.

You may be a computer programmer. Or you may be a man-child. While some women like the juvenile look, if you want to be taken more seriously, try to pair up those T-shirts with interesting vintage suit jackets, make sure those jeans actually fit (not too baggy or too tight) and get rid of the throwbacks. Also, depending on what kind of woman (or career) you're trying to attract, a suit might be a good investment.

It's all workout clothes and pajama jeans.

Comfort for you is king (or queen), but you have to be careful. It's easy to cross over from looking relaxed to looking lazy. You want to stand out. Wearing your plaid pajama bottoms to the grocery store may give the impression to potential friends and suitors that you're (a) a new parent suffering from severe exhaustion who can't be bothered to dress properly, (b) a broke college student who thinks the world is your parents' basement or (c) unemployed.

Take a step back and look at yourself and ask—would you date you wearing that? Remember, if you have a high standard of how you expect your date to look, you should probably dress to attract someone of that standard. Dressing for success in love means knowing your audience—and your personal style.

CHAPTER 7

No Mean Muggin'

When Alisha first came to New York City after spending most of her life in the Midwest she was puzzled. Every guy she met seemed to think she was flirting with them. She'd get on the bus and say hello to the bus driver and he'd ask for her number. She'd ask someone for directions and they'd assume she was available. She'd look over at someone walking her way and nod and they'd stop whatever they were doing to run over and ask for her number.

"Gee, the men sure are aggressive here," she thought.

Then, one particularly uncomfortable day, while walking past some garbage men doing their pickup, they made eye contact with her, stopped the truck and got out to approach her. Alisha realized this was going beyond odd and veering into uncomfortable/creepy territory. But when she talked to her coworkers they griped that men were rarely this friendly or aggressive to them. Alisha was no older or younger than her co-workers. Some were conventionally much more attractive, even. She mentioned this offhandedly to her boss, who was also from the Midwest, who was easily able to pinpoint Alisha's sudden new irresistibility.

"You smile," he said.

The boss, who had lived for some time on the East Coast, pointed out that East Coasters aren't nearly as "smiley" or friendly toward complete strangers as Southerners or Midwesterners. Alisha was doing what she'd always done—smiling out of kindness and courtesy—but on the East Coast people, especially women, seemed to only smile if they were obviously flirting (or at least available and open to flirting). By just being the Midwestern version of "nice," she was signaling to a multitude of random men that she was interested when, clearly, she was not. She was just being nice.

And so, Alisha, like countless women who'd moved to the East Coast and had to deal with the awkward/scariness of random men following them, confusing "nice" with "available," stopped smiling. For anyone.

When she walked outside, she kept her eyes low or distracted. She put in headphones when on the subway or the bus. She kept herself preoccupied with a book or her iPad when in public. She learned to ignore just about any kind of interaction with any stranger, until she was almost always living completely in her own head when in public no matter what was going on around her.

While this was great for keeping at bay creepy guys she didn't want entering her personal space, it also had the added effect of making her unapproachable to anyone. Arms folded firmly against her chest, refusing to look anyone in the eye, clearly signaled "leave this woman alone," even during times when Alisha might have wanted to talk to someone. After a few years of East Coast living, Alisha was struggling to make new friends and get dates, largely because of her imposing, unfriendly body language. But was there a way to make her appear more open and receptive to the people she wanted to meet without inviting the attention of everyone?

It's understandable why women like Alisha, and countless others, walk around looking mad. The creepily aggressive street harassers have created a hostile environment for a lot of women, making it easier to simply be unapproachable to everyone, rather than accidentally invite the attention of creeps. The problem with this is that by making yourself unapproachable you cut off your chances of meeting many wonderful, well-adjusted, interesting people who think you'd rather not be bothered and respect your desire for space. How do you strike that balance?

In a perfect world, there would be no street harassment. Many men who do this don't realize that for women, there's no way to tell the difference between lighthearted joking and the approaches that come from men who would try to harm them. Rather than try to figure out which guys are just joking around and which would actually try to assault them, women simply put their guard up with everyone. It's an unfortunate part of our reality. Alisha, after all, didn't want to have to stop smiling at people, but often the onus on not becoming an assault victim is put on women, not for perpetrators to stop harassing and/or assaulting.

But because we don't live in a perfect world and our body language speaks volumes, in order to meet new people and make ourselves more available for love, we have to "stop mean mugging" and find a way to be approachable while still maintaining our safety and space.

For Alisha, it wasn't just her smiling that made random men think she was interested, it was that her body language gave conflicting messages—in some cases signals of uncertainty, nervousness and weakness—that made her vulnerable, attracting men who felt they could pressure her into giving a phone number or physical contact.

Alisha would smile, but her eyes would widen with uncertainty. Her eyebrows would sometimes pitch up and squeeze together, signaling fear when she was uncomfortable with men who approached her. She would clasp her hands tightly in front of her on the bus and would try to make herself seem smaller by crossing her legs or ankles and shrugging her shoulders in.

Everything about how she walked, from her posture (often slouched, even though Alisha was 5'3") to her tendency to want to take up as little space as possible, made her seem unsure of herself and conflicted. This sense of weakness, coupled with her friendly smile, made it seem like she was vying for approval from the strange men she met on the street. And they misinterpreted this look of desiring approval with her wanting to curry their favor or interest.

Smiling was a very small part of a much bigger problem for Alisha. The big city made her nervous and her body language was full of nervous gestures. Tossing a smile on top just made it worse. And while no one could confuse her crossed arms and feet and a scowl on top for openness, she still had all those same habits of trying to make herself smaller. She looked scared and nervous. She looked uncomfortable. And this look ran contrary to Alisha's core personality.

Alisha—outgoing, warm, intelligent and affable—was a winner at work, often projecting confidence and empathy. It was hard to reconcile how someone who seemed so sure of herself when giving a presentation or meeting with clients could turn into a mess of bad body language when on the subway or walking down the street, or when she was at a club or restaurant or any event with a large number of strangers. Subconsciously, the more people around Alisha didn't know, the more she wanted to blend in and be invisible. It was a bad habit left over from years being teased as a child in public school. She'd learned how to make herself "invisible" to bullies. But this had a detrimental effect on her ability to meet new people in New York.

And a lot of people are like Alisha.

Author and body language expert Janine Driver runs down the many ways people like Alisha (educated and talented, bright but introverted and struggling with interpersonal skills) shoot themselves in the foot with bad posture and bad habits. In her book *You Say More Than You Think*, Driver outlines how their body language is mostly out of habit, telling on their old insecurities and faults.

"Some of us are lucky—we're born with an effortless way of interacting with other people. Natural charm, you might call it. Or charisma. But many of us need to work to uncover this natural charm within ourselves," Driver writes.

Just a few changes could easily move them from being not confident toward being self-assured and approachable but still in control enough to demonstrate they're not easy pickings for those who would try to take advantage.

Cribbing from Driver's lessons and using Alisha as an example—here's how she moved from looking like a nervous Midwesterner to a confident charmer.

Stop touching yourself—Alisha would chronically fidget in public. She felt she needed to do something with her hands in order to seem "preoccupied," but far too often what she chose to do made her look nervous. Alisha would stare at her fingernails, hug herself, thrust her hands into her pockets, cover her neck with her hand or cross her arms. All these gestures signaled that she was uncomfortable, stressed or sad.

Stop shrugging—When in settings with large groups of unfamiliar people, like a party or event, Alisha had a habit of shrugging in response to questions. Shrugging is a sure sign of uncertainty. Again, it made her seem unsure and weak.

Open up your physicality—This means putting your hands at your sides or both hands on your hips in a Superman pose to convey openness, confidence and strength. Stand up straight, don't try to cover or touch any vulnerable areas of yourself—like your neck. Look who you're talking to in the eye and position yourself toward them. In Driver's book she discusses the Belly Button Rule, where if someone's belly button is turned toward you it's good—it means they're interested or open to speaking to you. But if they're facing you and their belly button is facing away, something is wrong. By facing forward, keeping our hands at our sides or on both hips, we are conveying confidence and power, while still being approachable.

By removing the conflicting nervous gestures, Alisha found she could smile like the typical Midwesterner she was without getting the unwanted attention of aggressive suitors. Alisha's confident, warm smiles were now followed up with a commanding, self-assured body language that signaled her smiles were just that—smiles—and not an invitation.

But it didn't stop at just that for Alisha. Once she got her confidence gestures right and eliminated her slouching, self-touching and aversion for eye contact, she got into learning how to use body language to get the right response from people she wanted to potentially date or befriend.

This meant that same self-confidence but with a twist.

When Alisha was at a party or a bar, and was enjoying the company of a man who approached her, she would lean toward him, her belly button would be turned toward him; if she crossed her legs, she would even cross her legs in the handsome gent's direction. She would carefully touch or play with her own hair while smiling and listening to what he had to say. And if she touched the man, she would do a "grab and release," as described in Driver's book. She would gently grip his forearm or bicep to get his attention, hold for three seconds, then let go. During introductory handshakes, she would sometimes rest her left hand on top of both their hands, effectively sandwiching the man's hand between her own. All the while she kept her body language open and maintained eye contact.

Alisha found she needed less and less to ever "mean mug" to make a point for the "bad" strangers to stay away. Her confidence projected that she would likely be far too much trouble for anyone up to no good. Her confidence commanded respect and that's what she was treated with.

Even her smile and how she chose to use it told the story of what level of contact she wanted. A no-teeth, terse, tight-lipped smile signaled disinterest, contempt or that Alisha wanted a conversation to quickly end. A toothy, wide smile where her eyes would look away rather than at the person she was supposed to be smiling at displayed that the conversation was ending and she was moving on. A polite smile with teeth where her eyes remained placid and unchanged seemed professional and impersonal. But if Alisha had a big, genuine smile where her eyes "smiled" as well, crinkling up and squinting, it was almost as if Alisha were smiling at a close friend or relative. Naturally, the most genuine smile she reserved for those close to her often worked best when she met a potential friend or suitor.

Suddenly the men Alisha liked seemed to be more available and pick up on her signals faster. She also found that in better understanding her own body language, she could better read that of the men and women she met. She was able to tell who wanted to chat and who didn't, who was interested and who wasn't. Who could become a potential friend or paramour in just an initial meeting or glance. It was like Alisha had a superpower to read the emotions of strangers.

But it's a superpower any of us can learn.

After all, in the world of romance, you can't, as the film *Jerry Maguire* taught us, "have someone at hello" if you don't say hello and smile first.

Make yourself feel more confident by "faking it before you make it." Next time you feel nervous or insecure in a public setting, adopt this stance—no matter what—and tell yourself you are secure.

1. Stand up straight.

2. Place your hands on your hips or hook your thumbs into your pockets or belt loops. Avoid shoving your hands completely into your pockets or crossing your arms. Keep that body language open!

3. Look those you greet in the eye.

4. Give a firm but gentle handshake that interlocks your right thumb with theirs when you shake, and give a slight, gentle squeeze for warmth.

5. Smile!

6. Give good B.B.R. (Belly Button Rule).

7. When you introduce yourself and the

person you're greeting says his name, repeat his name back at him, "Hi, Charles, it's nice to meet you." Keep the focus on listening to what the person you just met had to say—not on yourself. After all, you're here to meet new people, not obsess over whether you said hello right.

8. If you forget the name midconversation, ask for a business card when it's time to exchange information, then jot down a description of who you just met on the back to help you remember their name. If they don't have a card, ask them to spell their name for you. Repeat back the name after you write it down to help you remember it.

When we carry ourselves in a confident manner—even if internally we aren't there yet—we can train our brains to see ourselves differently and match our inside emotions with what our outside body is doing. Correct the comfort gestures and get open!

CHAPTER 8

The (Instant) Message Should Match the Method

To text or not to text? That is the question.

A long time ago, like the early 2000s, after a date it was pretty typical for either you or your date to reach out via a phone call a day or two afterward. It was a great way of knowing if you'd (a) both enjoyed the date and (b) would see each other again.

So now, when you get that text message a few hours after your date saying "GR8 time 2-nite!" does that count the same as the phone call of a few years prior? Is a text a response or a toss-off line? And what does it mean if your date didn't even take the time to spell out words? And does this mean you call now since they texted first?

We're dating in the future now. The bar of communication is lower yet somehow ever more confusing.

If you're under thirty, texting is probably your favorite (and best) mode of instant communication. You probably text a lot and often. You probably text more than you talk on a phone. It's quick. It's easy. And it involves none of the investment or dedication of a phone call that could last anywhere from two minutes to two hours.

If you're over thirty, you were probably really annoyed that your date couldn't be bothered to write out the word "great" instead of "GR8" in that "What on Earth was that supposed to mean?" cryptic text. But even by now, post-thirtysomething, you've found texting to be somewhat useful. Like if you're running late to meet with someone or if you need a confirmation or a quick answer to a question. It's not surprising that some folks—especially those who don't care for talking on the phone, or introverts who prefer impersonal and informal communications like texts or instant messaging chats because it cuts down on uncomfortable physical interactions—love the many new, different ways we can communicate without talking or being face-to-face. The only problem is that when dating, how you choose to interface can directly impact your dating life—both negatively and positively. A conversation too casual can leave someone thinking you're not interested. But a conversation too formal or closed off can get you that exact same, uninterested result.

It's understandable to know what's appropriate and what's not appropriate now that more than 38 percent of mobile phone users are smartphone users. There are more than ninety million people in the United States (a country of over three hundred million) walking around armed with a device more computer than phone, all texting, tweeting, Facebooking and e-mailing along with occasionally making or receiving a good old-fashioned phone call.

Post-date communication has never been easier . . . to screw up.

The Text

UPSIDE: Great for quick communications, the text for many introverts has become the communication of choice. No more long, meandering conversations where you forget why you called. You get what you want, when you want, right away and to the point. Need to know what time to meet there? Shoot a text. Need to know the address? Shoot a text. Need to say you'll be a few minutes late? Text! Text! Text!

And since everyone seems to have their phone with them all the time these days, it's as close as you can get to 24/7 instant messaging without being chained to your laptop.

DOWNSIDE: When you need to really explain yourself, declare your feelings, clear up a misunderstanding or show you care—texting can fall short. After all, it's a pretty limited form of communication. Prattle on too long in a text and your recipient may wonder why you didn't just pick up the phone. But using it for a quick response for an important moment where a conversation is warranted can make it seem like you're avoiding someone. You may dash off a text after that first date to say you had a "GR8 time!" and made it home OK, but that shouldn't take the place of a more detailed form of communication if you want to go out again.

The E-mail

UPSIDE: It's like a letter—but faster and free. No need to wait for the postal service and no need for stamps. You can say as much (or as little) as you'd like. And you can make any e-mail as formal or informal as you may need. Good enough for job applications and keeping up with your long-distance friends alike. Post-date it's a great way to get more in-depth—in writing.

DOWNSIDE: Depending on how your date uses e-mail, it's either a staple of their lives or just a place where spam piles up. Maybe they read your note? Maybe they only use that e-mail addy to collect junk mail from the many services and accounts they sign up for online. Unlike texting, it's not a guarantee they'll read what you wrote and respond with any quickness. Never mind that if you're new to your date's life, that e-mail could wind up in the spam folder and they may never see it at all. Plus, an e-mail when you're getting to know each other can feel really impersonal and lacks immediacy.

The Instant Message

UPSIDE: It's almost as good as talking! In real time, you can have typed conversations that can go as short or as long as you'd like. And like a spoken conversation, you can go deep and learn a lot about each other. It's easy to become best-instant-messaging buddies with a friend, using the tool to keep the conversation going while at work during the day—all without alarming your employer.

DOWNSIDE: Not everyone is an IM fan. Like with e-mail, you have to be logged into that account to get those messages, and if your paramour isn't constantly attached to a laptop or desktop computer during the day, IM may seem more cumbersome than conversational. There's also a danger if you both love IM and you've only met virtually—through Facebook or a dating site. You can have all these wonderful, complex, in-depth IM chats, only to learn there's zero chemistry when you meet in person. The same tool that can bond a relationship closer and quicker can prolong a relationship that would never work IRL, aka "in real life."

The Tweet

UPSIDE: Like the text and the IM, it's how instant it is that makes it so valuable. For quick convos, it's great.

DOWNSIDE: Where do we start? You only get 140 characters to make your point. If your paramour doesn't "follow" you on the service, you can't send them private messages. If they do follow you and you can send private messages, there's a chance they're one of the millions of folks who start a Twitter account and never, ever check it again. Also, Twitter isn't very private. Whatever you tweet, chances are you're sharing it with the world. Twitter is a great marketing tool if you're a blogger, celebrity or someone with something to sell. For the rest of us, it falls flat. Twitter is often a one-way conversation between a dedicated self-promoter and his or her fans. Not so great for romance. Tweeting your love is probably the least serious (yet public) way you could ever go about it.

The Book of Faces

UPSIDE: Everyone is on Facebook. The most popular social networking tool today, many folks have eschewed joining online dating services and just use Facebook for all dating and professional networking. It's an incredible tool. Photos, videos, personal info, ways to communicate both using instant messaging and e-mail—Facebook is one of the more useful and personally addictive forms of social networking. After all, years ago you might not have had a relationship with your friends from Girl Scouts or your third cousin once removed on your father's side at all. But Facebook brings us all together, keeps us all in touch, just one status update away.

DOWNSIDE: Everyone is on Facebook. And the constantly changing privacy controls make it less and less private and personal each day. And while you may be a prolific Facebooker, there are many other people who barely use the service. Also, because of the "private" nature of how you can adjust your security controls on FB, if you act too familiar or personal on someone's Facebook page it can scare them off. Say "Great date" by posting it to their timeline and they'll think you're creepy, broadcasting their personal business to the world. Say "Great date" in a FB e-mail or chat and they may never see it because they don't like using FB e-mail or chat. And while you may learn a lot about your date by researching their background on FB, to start spouting that off before you get to know each other in real life can be off-putting. If you decide to use your insider knowledge to ask them about their divorce or battle with muscular dystrophy on the first date, you may never, ever get a second one. Even if their lives are public knowledge, the rules of courtship deem that nothing is real until it comes from their lips. Complex life issues should be brought up by the person living through them when they're ready to talk about them—not just because you saw that they have a kid on FB.

The thing to remember with all our modes of communication—Don't. Over. Analyze.

Sometimes a text, Tweet or status update is just that. If you check your date's FB status the next day and find them lamenting people being uncaring, don't just assume that's about you. That could be about their boss or their mother or a friend they're feuding with. You can't assume that every online lament is about you—especially if it's a public whine.

Also, for those less astute and comfortable with communication, texting is a way to keep from being misunderstood. It's important to gauge your date's comfort zone when it comes to communication. The more introverted they are, the more they may prefer interpersonal forms of social networking. But even this isn't a hard and fast rule. Remember Alisha from chapter 7? She's an introvert, but she despises texting because she can't type very fast on her smartphone. Texting is the last way she ever wants to have a conversation even though many of her friends and the men she dates prefer to text. They think she's being rude or uncaring when she shoots back a one- or two-word text. But if you sit her in front of a keyboard, she can give you the world. She just really hates texting.

So, again, not about you. Not an indictment of you if someone doesn't text back right away. With so many communication choices, people are bound to have preferred methods.

One woman's beloved texts are another man's darling e-mails.

Don't sweat it if you end up falling for someone who thinks Skype (the video chat, phone and instant messaging service) is the end-all, be-all in modern communication.

Don't be hard on yourself if—for you—Skype isn't.

Also, if you're exploring better relationship building through online communication, remember—what you type or how you type says a lot about who you are.

Poor grammar, spelling or punctuation? For the grammar snob, you might get labeled as unintelligent even though in real life you're a well-respected businessperson or graduate student.

ALL CAPS? **WHY ARE YOU SHOUTING AT ME?** ALL CAPS make you sound angry and are tough for anyone to read for any length of time. It's best to be avoided.

2 MUCH TXT SPK? Maybe if you're under thirty you won't get penalized for not wanting to completely spell out words, but that's a big maybe. For many people, TXT SPK (or "text speak") is too informal. Save it for your good friends who already know you know how to spell.

The key with communication is that even though we have more methods than ever to reach out, do not lose sight that these are just tools. Our goal, always, is for our intentions to be clear and for us to be understood. Work the communication tools that work best for you. And remember, no amount of online chatter can take the place of face-to-face contact. At some point we have to get off-line and get serious.

Texting, tweeting and using Facebook are meant to enhance our overall communication, not replace human interaction. If your goal is to find love, at some point you have to get out from behind your laptops and smartphones and get into reality.

Taking cues from the different forms of communication listed in this chapter, learn what form is your preferred method of communication and what this says about you.

TEXT: You don't like to talk. In fact, your favorite thing to say is why should you call someone if you can just text? But sometimes it's hard for you to remember that texting your mother "Happy B-Day" doesn't take the place of a card, gift or an actual conversation.

E-MAIL: You like to write, but you also like to avoid people. Maybe you're afraid of their response and that's why you send questions and important notes to those you know through a channel they may or may not check with much frequency.

INSTANT MESSAGE: You love the feel of a good conversation with the aid of a laptop keyboard and a way to distract yourself at work. You also may just love to write out your thoughts, believing that you're a better communicator this way and better at expressing how you feel without being misunderstood. The only downside is that the lack of actual face-to-face chat time may be impacting your interpersonal social skills. No matter how fast a typist you are, you can't conduct an entire relationship through instant messaging. Learn how to express yourself—vocally.

TWEET: You're a teenager aren't you? Because if you and your friends are always on Twitter, it might make sense as a mode of conversation. But if you're an adult trying to date someone it's best to be avoided.

FACEBOOK: Great for connecting with old class-mates and coworkers but might feel a little odd or impersonal to someone you're dating who has your cell phone number and e-mail address and wonders why you didn't just call, text, IM, or e-mail them first.

Ask yourself: How do you feel when someone sends you an important message over a social networking site or via texting? Is there ever a time when it's not appropriate?

CHAPTER 9

Move Online to Off-line, Quickly

James was really good at this online dating thing. Too good.

He treated PerfectMatch.com, OkCupid and the like no different from how we would treat a meal at Old Country Buffet. Everywhere he saw an endless delight of dateable women, right at his fingertips. He drafted spreadsheets and calendars to keep track of them all. He was rarely ever alone on any given night. It was endless conquest for him, the endless game. How quickly could he go from shopping through pages upon pages of photos of women, to quick e-mails and phone chats to dates and then the bedroom?

He couldn't believe such a tool was so widely available and so free. And how freeing it was to use it.

Until he found himself listed on Don't Date Him Girl—a website for serial cheats and liars.

While James felt his profile getting blown up on cheater sites was unfair—James had no "serious" girlfriend, after all, just a series of romantic partners he juggled—the hurt the women he pursued online was real. They felt he had an unfair advantage in that he wasn't using sites like PerfectMatch or eHarmony for love—but to fill his rotating sexual schedule. And that much was true. He had taken a system that allowed him to present the best of him—his handsome photo, his exciting life, his career, his earner status and his charm in five hundred words or less—as an advertisement for the "perfect guy." And he had gamed the system in his favor. And he'd converted his online encounters into off-line dates. But running into a guy like James wasn't that much fun for Emily, who thought she'd selected a date with a charming, puckish banker and ended up having sex with the human merry-go-round of Washington, D.C.

But Emily was always going to be a good mark for someone like James. Someone who spent her high school and college and her twenties focusing on her education and career. Someone who her parents—with her being their only child—sheltered, who did not date until she was twenty-five and now only dated sporadically. Someone who, despite not being a virgin, might as well have been. But while she'd studied for her SATs and for the bar exam and studied up on her cases as a lawyer, she hadn't given much thought to how to navigate the world of dating—let alone dating online.

She always thought dating online was something desperate people did. But after living in D.C. for five years and being without a date the last four, she realized she needed to do something different. Yet, like so many before, she'd fallen into James's obvious trap. Why didn't she see through the flattery and the big talk? Why didn't she know he wasn't serious?

Because Emily had practiced and studied for her career but not for love, and everyone needs practice.

While we'll occasionally meet someone who is preternaturally sophisticated in the world of making friends, dating and mating (like James), most of us learn how to interact the old-fashioned way—by trial and humiliation. But that never happened to Emily. Her parents had worried about her getting pregnant in high school, so they never allowed her to date. Then Emily continued to have some variation of this fear in college and focused intently on her studies.

By the time we met, Emily was in her thirties and had never been in a serious relationship, never dated anyone longer than a month and was perplexed.

When I suggested the online dating world she frowned.

She tried that once and met James.

Obviously online dating was the problem.

But it wasn't.

It was Emily's attitude.

Emily needed a place to practice, to finally hone those skills on dating and mating that she had never developed in high school or college. She needed to stop expecting perfection out of herself when it came to a skill she'd never developed.

Online dating isn't something to fear. It is a tool, the ultimate practice ground. A place to build confidence and a great place to better understand your wants and needs.

Online is where you have the same thing James realized he had—control.

Hundreds of years of social conditioning had told Emily the path to love was passive for a woman— she was to sit and wait for love to approach her. Online she'd done the same. She put up an earnest and sweet profile, showcasing a favorite photo, and expected to sift through whatever inquiries came her way from interested men, finally selecting the one most appealing to her.

Instead, Emily's sweet profile was bombarded by messages from our friend from chapter 5, the man who didn't care about the word "no." Emily, an at-

tractive woman, was inundated with short messages—
what I call the "shotgun" technique that allows men
to make up in volume what they lose in accuracy—
from men who sent "winks" and flirtations to any
and every woman regardless of compatibility. They
didn't read profiles. They didn't care about Emily's
"interests." If they liked her photo, they fired off a
message and sometimes the message was misspelled
and vulgar.

So many of the men who approached her online
seemed incompatible or beyond what she was looking for that when James—of good spelling, education, employment and charm—came along, she
ignored all the obvious signs that he wasn't serious.

This technique, one that many women fall for
online, does no one any service, especially the
woman on the receiving end of this avalanche of unwanted and inaccurate attention. Emily was a sniper
to their shotgun technique, carefully and obsessively
choosing who to message. But if you're a woman
and using an online dating service, being obsessive
is pointless.

Remember how in chapter 5 I said we have to
get over the word "no"? That was the word "no"
when it came to meeting people in person. If you're
afraid of rejection from people you never see face-
to-face, people you see anonymously in an online
dating profile, you have a problem.

This is the lowest interaction point you can have online. There is little to no chance of public humiliation. And finally, we're all in control of who we want to approach and who can approach us. The woman who realizes her power in online dating—and takes advantage of it—is the woman who has the best online dating experience.

If you're having a bad time dating online, chances are it's because you haven't taken control.

If the rules of sexism work against you in approaching a man in the public space, they work for you online. The most aggressive woman online gets the most dates.

Every. Time.

And the statistics back it up.

According to the dating site OkCupid, 40 percent of female-to-male messages get a response. So for someone successful and good-looking like James, approaching women aggressively online first makes sense; for women it makes a lot more sense. James is a bit of an anomaly. The whole point of a man messaging women by the volume is that most won't respond at all, but all you need are a few yes responses to make up for a barrage of nos. But with a 40 percent chance of a reply, the aggressive woman is the one who gets the most dates.

Women like Emily should treat online dating as a way to prescreen those she's potentially interested in, picking among the men she finds attractive or interesting or compatible, then sending them a brief message to get the conversation going. While it's true the man Emily may message might look at her photo then decide not to pursue, what happens more often than not is the man will write back, intrigued by this validation of their look or overall profile.

What was ironic about Emily, for all her inexperience in dating and men, was that she had an outstanding online profile, avoiding many of the mistakes that cause others to pass over profiles. Emily had a great photo—just like the photos we discussed in chapter 6—she smiled, she addressed the camera, she came across as lovely, personable and flirty, all while emphasizing her best features in a three-quarter profile. Ninety percent of whether you get a reply comes down to your photo, and Emily understood how to take a nice photo from years of practice, figuring out her best angle and positioning because she feared awkward "candid" photos of her surfacing on sites like Facebook due to shutter-happy friends. She'd long since taken the time to figure out her best side and angles. It was rare that she took a bad photo if she knew a camera was present.

Emily was also a good writer. She made sure her written profile was devoid of spelling and grammatical errors that might make her seem less intelligent than she was. She was meticulous in filling out the profile, covering all the necessary areas without being too wordy, and she stayed away from "no" statements—negative statements that made her seem bitter, angry or unapproachable. Potential dates always respond better to the positive "I love Thai food," than a list of dislikes—"No short guys. No beer bellies. No one with less than a master's degree."

But dating sites aren't the only online tools you can utilize to improve your dating chances—the World Wide Web is your playground.

How often have you met someone who seemed interesting and you immediately searched for them on Google? Perhaps they were a potential coworker or employer? Maybe they were the date your sister brought home? Maybe it was a new friend you were thinking of going into business with?

Using an online search engine is the fastest way to find out background information on a stranger. Every day more and more info is available online—from court records to past employment—that helps you screen the individuals you meet in your life. A quick check on Facebook allows you to discover someone's age or relationship status. A glance at networking sites like LinkedIn gives you a clue on employment information and educational background.

And the more people you know, both in real life and online, the more people you meet. And the more people you meet, the more opportunities you have to meet the person right for you. Studies show that people with the widest social circles date and marry more often than loners.

But once you make these online connections you can't waste time online with them. It's easy to relate to someone when the interaction risk is low—an e-mail here, an instant messaging chat there. The only way to find out if you're truly compatible or possess that ever-elusive thing called "chemistry" is to meet in person.

Part of the reason why Emily was so negative about online dating was because many years ago, in the early days of online dating—the 1990s—Emily had met a "nice" guy online. They talked on the phone for hours and chatted constantly through e-mail and in online chat rooms. She quickly started having feelings for him as they seemed to have so much in common. The couple didn't meet until six months after their first online correspondence, but as soon as Emily saw the young man get off the bus and walk toward her, she knew she made a mistake.

While she knew everything about him—from his family history to his desire to be a professional chef—the young man's posture, personal hygiene, body language and appearance was contrary to any guy she would have ever found attractive. On top of that, while he had been talkative and funny online, he was quiet and insecure in person. He was a terrible dud, but because of her promise she was stuck with him for a whole, unpleasant weekend.

He was heartbroken after he returned to his home out of state and Emily refused to return his calls or e-mails. And she felt ashamed, but she couldn't go out with him. He, if she was honest about her feelings, personally disgusted her. But they had spent six months talking, bonding, getting to know each other.

Only to learn that on Emily's end it would never, ever work.

Nearly two decades later, little has changed. The introverted can be outgoing online. The insecure can be confident. But all truth is revealed once you meet in person. It's so much harder to hide our flaws, hence . . . if you're dating online you have to eventually date—in person. The only way you'll ever know if you're investing in a potentially valuable relationship or wasting time is to meet in person. And you should do this while the burden and expectations are low. Once you realize someone has potential, schedule a quick meeting for coffee and conversation—not a full-fledged dress-up date but just an in-person chat—and then decide if there's more to develop. You'll find what works in theory often works much differently in practice.

If Emily had agreed to a coffee date with James, maybe she wouldn't have put so many expectations and pressure on it. A quick conversation over a chai latte would have revealed James wasn't looking for anything serious. She could have quickly asked and learned that he was out to have fun and had no interest in long-term commitment or marriage.

Instead she and James met on a high-stakes first date of dinner and drinks, where she got all dressed up, and expectations, for her, were very high. She'd read so much about James's career and interests and talents in his profile and in their initial online conversations, she felt an incredible pressure to "get" James because he sounded like such a catch. She was already at an emotional disadvantage before the appetizers came out. She wanted to impress him and please him, not picking up on James's obvious gamesmanship, his obvious desire to "score" over getting to know her.

If Emily had met James for a very casual coffee date, she would have quickly learned he preferred drinks because alcohol lowered inhibitions. In thirty minutes she would have noticed that he spent more time checking his BlackBerry than looking her in the eye. She would have noticed that his answers to her questions were paper thin, that he wasn't emotionally invested in anyone and couldn't see past her doe-like brown eyes or curvy figure. And she would have had control, in picking a public, centrally located coffee shop where pressure was low and expectations were too. If James had really wanted to get to know her, he would have relished the conversation. But James only wanted fun and control over that fun, which is why he picked the bar, why he insisted on driving when they'd only spoken a few times, why he picked a place far outside of her comfort zone.

James was a shark who had designs to sharpen his teeth on her, and she was far too green to know any better. Which was why she spent days obsessing over why all she'd received from him since their date was an anemic text message and silence, while other women James dated picked up on his modus operandi quickly. More experienced than she, other women knew it was a game and laughed it off, moved on.

Comedian Chris Rock said it best: When you meet somebody for the first time, you're not meeting them. You're meeting their representative. James could pretend to be a "nice guy" looking for something serious for a little while, but he was impatient. Whether on- or off-line, he didn't have the time or interest to get to know anyone. Conquest to the next—that was his motto—all hidden behind smiles and false modesty.

Here are some tips on how to quickly make that move from online to off-line to avoid wasting your time:

- Don't overconcern yourself with a written profile—the key is to see if you're attracted to their photo and if they list any non-starters in their profile (like not wanting children, or a religious preference that is incompatible with your own).

- Next, send a message. It doesn't have to be a long dissertation, just something succinct about your interest in them. Brevity is key!

- When a response comes back, use your gut. Do you want to go to the next step? As long as the response isn't something off-putting or scarily vulgar (one of my clients once said a man responded to her message by professing his love for eating chicken and oral sex on a first date), you can move on to the next phase. And don't fret too much if it takes them a bit longer than twenty-four hours to get back to you. Not everyone stays logged into the dating site at all hours, but check it every week or so.

- Immediately invite the person to call but remember safety; you can use a private line, blocked number or you can make the call over the Internet using a free service like Google Talk.

- Make sure to use the phone conversation as another way to determine whether this person is ideal to invite out to an impromptu, informal, public coffee date. Monitor their response—if they have a hard time nailing down a time for thirty minutes' worth of Starbucks, that's a bit of a red flag. Typically people who seem overloaded are exaggerating to hide that they're married or otherwise occupied.

- Keep the coffee date to thirty minutes or less and use it to determine if you want a "full first date."

Moving from online to off-line should be fun. This was the message I tried to get through to Emily. By taking control of her dating life, establishing good boundaries, not wasting time online, meeting in safe places for preliminary coffee dates, listening to her gut, she could get caught up in the experience she missed out on when she was younger. Online dating could be the boot camp she needed to get back out there and get what she wanted. But she had to make sure she felt safe. She had to give herself the room and permission to make mistakes and learn from them. She had to learn that dating was something she allowed to happen to her and something she made happen with the men she wanted.

She had to create her own strategy for dating online and moving it off-line, all while remaining safe and confident. Online dating gives you control.

Technology makes meeting people easier, but at some point you still have to meet—in person.

Following the steps outlined in the chapter, get started on developing your own profile and seeking out others to message online. Keep a record of your interactions so that you can learn from your experiences what worked for you and what didn't.

CHAPTER 10

You Will Be "Googled"

Emily was overly protective. This was why even though she was weak in gauging interest or seriousness due to her lack of experience in dating, she was good at protecting her image and profile online.

Emily was hyperaware of not putting too much personal information on the Web and utilizing sites like Facebook and LinkedIn in ways that helped her personally and in her career, but didn't make her vulnerable to those who may exploit the information they'd learn about her.

Emily expected to be googled. She knew there was no such thing as privacy online.

She was the exact opposite of Lance.

Lance, as his name should hint toward, is a man. And like most men he wasn't raised to think much beyond his personal safety than to avoid being robbed in less-than-savory neighborhoods. As a man, he didn't fear most women no matter their size or level of influence. He wasn't too worried about stalking or personal safety outside of keeping his wallet in places pickpockets couldn't take advantage of. Otherwise he did what he wanted. Take the subway all hours of the night. Walk ten blocks home drunk from the bar. Give out his number and personal information to attractive women he met. What damage could anyone really do to him? He was 6'3" and 225 pounds. He was more aware of how his imposing stature caused fear in others than of being afraid of what damage could be done to him.

But while Lance's size and masculinity protected him in public, it didn't do that much for him online. Because online, no one cared about his size or weight or height or physicality. He was a mark, as we all are, if we don't have control of our online profiles.

Lance's password on most sites was, quite woefully, "PASSWORD." On those that wouldn't allow him to get away with that, it was his last name plus the last two numbers of the year of his birth—77. He loved social networking—so many ways to meet and get to know others—but he wasn't big on staying up on privacy info. He rarely took advantage of privacy settings on Facebook. Anyone who was a "friend of a friend" could see his photos, his birthday, his places of employment. And Lance had tied his Twitter account to the site Foursquare—a site that allows you to earn points and badges for the number of times you frequent an establishment or place.

Lance didn't know this, but he was broadcasting where he was and who he was with 24/7. If you didn't figure out his password to his accounts was "PASSWORD," it was fairly easy to reset it. His high school, birthdate and mother's maiden name were all easy to find on his Facebook profile, which he didn't have protected.

Lance had no idea that Google is permanent. That every Tweet is presently being archived by the Library of Congress, that every blog is cached by Google—even if you delete it.

Lance didn't know that if he typed his first and last name into a search engine that the first thing that came up was a heavily biased rant by someone he barely knew, someone he had only met a few times and went on one date with who was eternally bitter toward him from her own circumstance.

He didn't know he was a target for simply doing nothing. He didn't know that even 6'3" tall men of 225 pounds were capable of having their reputations ruined by a tech-savvy malcontent.

In fact, Lance might not have ever known if it

weren't for Emily, who, after seeing his profile online, contacting him, having a few conversations with
him through instant message only to later google him
online and find a wealth of misinformation, told him
his online persona was compromised.

First of all, Emily discovered that while Lance—a
writer—had quite a handsome picture of himself on
his dating profile, once she learned his last name and
googled him, she found a plethora of ancient, drunken
party photos from the Google-based photo-sharing
site Picasa, Yahoo!'s photo-sharing site Flickr, and
some less secure accounts via his frat brothers on
Facebook.

Sure, the pictures were from Lance's college days
and were, in most cases, representative of someone
Lance hadn't been since he was nineteen, but with a
boyish look, and a few out-of-style fashions, who
would be the wiser? So many party pictures. Lance
doing body shots off women in Mexico. Lance passed
out. Lance shirtless and compromised. Emily was
worried she couldn't take him seriously, even though
Lance hadn't been that drunk in a decade, worked a
great job in advertising and was an otherwise responsible human being.

Then there was that old Myspace account from
college. Lance hadn't updated it in years, but it was
the first thing that came up when Emily googled him.
It reinforced the notion that Lance was some drunken

jerk, as it was filled with more party pictures, misspelled blog entries and immature accounts of his once wild life. It didn't reflect his volunteer work or steady career.

And then there was his stalker—the woman he'd only gone on one date with but who'd taken his rejection personally. Lance was an easygoing, sensitive guy. He hated to think he ever hurt anyone, but his stalker took his rejection above and beyond simple hurt feelings. Blog post after blog post detailed her hurt and his perceived shortcomings.

Lance's online persona was terrible. In so many ways he was lucky Emily wanted to talk to him at all.

He was also lucky that it hadn't affected his employment—unlike others who'd bounced from company to company, Lance had been with the same firm for years. But after Emily enlightened him on his messy profile, he realized he had a problem. It explained why he'd been passed over for jobs he'd applied for at more prestigious places.

One glance at his profile and anyone would be left with the impression that Lance was a messy, irresponsible person, not to be trusted. They knew nothing of his volunteer work, his mentoring of junior members of his fraternity, his affection toward his mother and sisters. They didn't know he was a responsible employee and highly moral man.

Online, Lance was a drunken frat boy, partying long after college ended.

It's important to take some control. Starting with:

Delete unused profiles: No one is on Myspace anymore, so why are you? If you can't update it, stay on top of it, be in control of it; that profile has to go.

Create your own profile: Don't have an online profile? Make one. Think of yourself as a celebrity with an unauthorized page on online encyclopedia *Wikipedia*. Sure, it's true that you were born in 1968, but did you want the world to know? Of course you enjoyed a particularly boozy trip to Cancun when you were twenty-one, but does all of Facebook need to know? Create your own profiles on social networking sites and archival sites, and maintain them. When someone searches for your name only the things you want should come up—not your tax lien from when you were twenty-five and bad with money.

Google yourself: Want to know what others are saying about you? At least once a month, do a search for yourself on various search engines and see what comes up. Inaccurate information can be fixed. Defamatory information can be dealt with. But if you don't know it's there, you can't counteract it at all. If you don't like searching for yourself, many sites like

Google will let you set up "alerts" that will search for your name and report whatever info they find on a daily, weekly or need-to-know basis.

Happy-go-lucky Lance was finally able to get control of his profile. It took a bit of work—building up profiles on sites that pop up higher on search engines and creating his own personal website so it would come up first instead of the complaints of his stalker—but it was doable.

Often getting rid of bad info was as simple as remembering his old Myspace login and password and deleting the profile or asking a friend on Facebook to remove irresponsible-looking pictures. Other things took a bit more work, like diluting the influence of his online stalker; but with his own page and social networking sites that he was in control of, it was only a matter of time before the stalker became more and more buried in any search. The key was Lance's taking control and fixing it so that no one could take advantage.

Because while his weight and height could impose upon potential troublemakers in public, the only way to stop identity thieves and malcontents online was to be the master of his own (Web) domain.

By seeking control online he found better control in his personal life and relationships.

Fortunately for Lance, after his thirty-minute

coffee date with Emily, she was able to assess he was a gentle giant, not a party boy. Fortunately it wasn't too late to fix what seemed to be out of control.

He could use the tools of the online world to benefit himself rather than be the victim of circumstance.

Got something online you need to get rid of? Try these techniques:

- For sites that post your personal information and address that they've grabbed from other places—like identity search sites such as PeekYou or Spokeo—contact the administrator directly to ask that your information be removed.

- Sign up for search engine alerts based on your name, nicknames or any other aliases people may be searching for you by, so when odd items with your name pop up you can screen them to see if it's something you need to contact a site about taking down. Google has such a service with its Google Alerts.

- Contact websites and their administrators directly if they are using your photos, words or information without your authorization.

- Create your own website using your name so that when people search for you they find what you want them to find first.

- Check your privacy settings on social networking sites like Facebook or LinkedIn to make sure you're only sharing information with the people you want to share information with.

- Delete or close old, unused social networking accounts. The last thing you want is your old Myspace profile from the early 2000s to come back to haunt you in unexpected ways.

- Do image searches for yourself along with keyword searches. If you find one of your images being used without permission, contact the site administrator.

- Close the comments on posts more than a year old if you have a weblog and delete old sites and blogs you haven't updated if the information on them no longer reflects your personal or professional life.

- Clean up old online photo accounts you may have on sites like Picasa, Photobucket or Flickr.

- Even if you don't use popular social networking sites like Facebook or Twitter, still register just so you have control over your name and so no one can create a fake account under your name, impersonating you.

- Purchase your name as a domain name if applicable. You never know where your life might take you and who might want to buy your name and use it for sketchy things.

CHAPTER 11

Sex Is Not Super Glue
(It Won't Make Him/Her Stick with You)

Michael was pretty sure he was the answer to every woman's problem—if all problems were in the bed-room.

He'd worked himself into becoming an ideal lover. He was tall, handsome, in excellent physical condition, charming, funny and disarming in a self-deprecating sort of way, even though he was 6'3" and didn't look like someone who had obvious flaws.

So if you didn't believe his little digs about how "clumsy" he was or how "unfortunate" in love he'd been, that was OK. Michael didn't believe it either. He seemed to be all but too pleased with himself, but understood you could get more out of people if you didn't seem so intimidating.

Poking fun at himself was one way to set everyone at ease.

And so for a long time, Michael enjoyed playing the field, believing that when it came time to settle down he'd have a bevy of options and many women to choose from. And while at first that seemed to be true, Michael found himself in a bind. He could find a woman—he had more than his fair share of girlfriends past and present and most of his relationships had ended on friendly terms—but he didn't feel strongly about anyone. They were all "nice," but they didn't seem right for him. And they all seemed to be obsessed with settling down with him, when he simply saw these "imperfect" potential brides as settling.

Then he met Lauryn. Smart, funny, gorgeous and talented, she was unlike any other woman he'd ever met. She'd enrolled in college at sixteen; she already had a postgraduate degree. She worked in scientific research, namely pharmaceuticals for a major university. Together, they had an electricity Michael hadn't felt with anyone else. She was disarming and unpredictable and seemed to know so much. It felt weird admitting it to his friends, but he liked that Lauryn was smarter and more sophisticated than he was. But there were obvious problems from the start, if Michael was honest. Lauryn was more than a decade younger than him (Michael had just turned forty while Lauryn was twenty-seven). She also had no interest in marriage or having children anytime soon—a reality Michael ignored, falling into the trap of believing that by virtue of Lauryn being a woman she would eventually want these things.

"Don't all women want to get married?" he'd say. He assumed Lauryn had expressed her desire for not wanting a husband or children as a way to impress him, ignoring the fact that her parents' marriage was a disaster that left her mother penniless and their family homeless for a year after the divorce. Lauryn had only recently started speaking to her father again after pretending he didn't exist since she was thirteen. He assumed that all women want to get married even though he was a child of divorce himself.

Which was Michael's secret pain, the source of his real problems. Not the ones he made up to make himself more approachable, but real, serious emotional problems that had kept him from bonding with past girlfriends. Michael's parents divorced when he was twelve and when his mother took a high-paying job in New York, he had a choice—move to the city with his mother or stay in Florida with his now depressed dad. Michael felt he couldn't leave his father, and even though he understood why his mother made the choice that she did, it still hurt. It still registered as abandonment and had stunted Michael's emotional growth.

He grew up tall and handsome but struggled with responsibility. Even though to this day, Michael continued to be closer to his mother than his father, that fear of her leaving him was still there, and it revealed itself in the women he chose to date rather than in the ones he had fallen in love with.

Michael found that he rarely dated any woman who was a real challenge to his heart. He bounced from pretty but bland girls, one after another, never emotionally investing. But the women he fell hard for reminded him of his career-driven, strong-willed mother, and in their shadows he felt inconsequential. He was obsessed with "proving" to them he was worth stopping whatever they were fixated on and taking notice. But not once had he been able to convert these complicated career women into making him their priority. It's a common psychological problem—trying to fix problems you have with your parents in the people you date.

Now ready to settle down, Michael hadn't chosen among the many pretty but nice girls he'd dated; he'd chosen the emotionally complicated, gorgeous and driven Lauryn—Lauryn who feared commitment and displayed many signs of not trusting Michael.

But because Michael had, for so long, feared a woman like Lauryn, he was always at an emotional disadvantage in the relationship. In his years of never going for what he wanted, he'd never learned to overcome his desire to please the type of girl Lauryn was, to his own detriment. Michael, a former skinny nerd and now a hunk, had confused being attractive and good in bed for real emotional intimacy. Meaning, Michael and Lauryn had amazing sex. Fiery, electric, passionate, crazy sex. And they had it, by his account, "all the time." But even with Lauryn, his dream girl, Michael struggled with emotional intimacy. He couldn't hold Lauryn's hand or hug her without wanting to bed her. He didn't understand a touch that didn't lead to the bedroom because he'd never been comfortable with non-sexual intimacy.

Michael didn't get that because he was so strong on sex and so weak on talking, affection and vulnerability, his dream girl, Lauryn, wasn't taking him seriously. He wanted to make her his wife, but she had no clue.

She thought she was just his sexual workout partner.

Michael, for all his strong feelings toward her, didn't exhibit any behavior that would cause Lauryn to see him as more than a fling. He joked around—a lot. Michael was rarely, if ever, serious about anything in conversation. He had a tendency to talk in stereotypes ("No man wants X, all women want Y") and, again, was disinterested in any emotional or physical intimacy that didn't lead to sex. When Lauryn had a bad day or was upset about something, she didn't bother telling Michael. The one time she tried to talk to him about her father and her mixed emotions toward him, Michael fell silent. He wasn't sure of what to say or do and was visibly uncomfortable. He never wanted to hold her hand in public. Any touching was a deliberate desire for sex. If Michael didn't want sex, he didn't even hug or kiss her hello.

And when she walked away from him after a year he was perplexed, fixated even. He had been so smitten, yet all she saw was a "friend with benefits." Michael didn't understand why she didn't take him seriously.

Out of all the muscles we're encouraged to exercise, our heart is often the one that gets the short shrift. We're taught that love "just happens." That through some magic we will find one another in this world and bond without conflict. And so many things that take work are chalked up to "nature." Then we punish ourselves for not "figuring out" what we think everyone else intrinsically just "knew."

But they didn't "know." Love is something most of us have to work out. It's rare for everything to happen so neat and cleanly—without trial and error. Without hurt feelings. Without consequence.

Michael had finally decided he wanted love, but all he got was what he'd always been able to get with little trouble—sex.

But great sex is hardly the building block of a long-lasting relationship. No matter how amazing the desire, as human beings, we can get used to anything. A pretty face eventually just becomes a pretty face. Sex is just sex. Physical attraction will get your foot in the door, but it's not a consistent indicator of if or when you will make a trip down the aisle.

Contrary to popular belief of what men want versus what women want—Michael had sex with Lauryn too early. And this isn't about some arbitrary thirty-, sixty- or ninety-day abstinence rule. Michael had sex with Lauryn before either was emotionally invested.

There are always consequences to having sex before emotional investment, and sexually transmitted diseases and unplanned pregnancy are examples. If both participants are on the same page, both in where the relationship is and where it may go—sex can be bonding, a building block. But if one partner is thinking of forever while the other is thinking of right now, having sex too soon can be a recipe for hurt feelings. Lauryn, like many women, had grown up in a society where women traditionally have borne the brunt of any and all negative opinions for having sex outside of marriage. Even though she was modern in her view of dating and intercourse, she still thought that having sex before any kind of commitment was a declarative statement of how serious the relationship is. Michael's desire and willingness to have sex with her within only a few weeks of knowing her signaled that Michael wasn't serious—even though he was. In the past, if or when Lauryn had sex with someone when they didn't know each other that well, it meant either one or both of them didn't see a future in the relationship.

Later on, Lauryn admitted to Michael that she was surprised he pursued her even after they'd had sex so quickly.

Adding to Lauryn's belief that Michael wasn't serious was that Michael talked about sex constantly—about his desire for it, his skill at it and the many, many women he'd bedded before. She knew about his reputation for conquest before they spent the night together and he never stopped talking about his popularity with women due to his looks and stamina long after they'd started dating. This added to her not taking him seriously. Who talks about the number of women they've bedded to a woman they're interested in? Lauryn asked. She got the impression very quickly that Michael wanted someone to temporarily share his bed with, not his life.

If you asked Michael about why he had sex so soon or why he talked about it so much with a woman he was seriously interested in he would have remarked that "sex is just sex."

But it isn't.

Sex wasn't just "sex," with Michael. He craved emotional intimacy but had channeled all that desire into sex. Lauryn remained tight-lipped about her number of partners out of fear of being judged. It seemed silly that either should have a "low" number—in the less-than-five category—when both were over twenty-five and had been sexually active since their late teens. Yet Lauryn felt a lot of pressure to keep her numbers "low" or to simply never broach the topic for fear it would foster insecurity in the men she dated. Responses to her sexual history ran the gamut from fearing they wouldn't measure up sexually to previous boyfriends or that she was "loose" or emotionally dysfunctional. Michael didn't get that while bragging about his "stats" was funny or admirable to his friends, to a potential girlfriend it was grating.

Also, while some can separate sex from love, I'd argue that they are the minority. For all the talk of male sexual proclivities, the statistical average number of sexual partners for a man in Michael's age range (thirty to forty-four) is seven. While Hollywood has glorified the sexual prowess of a tall, charming guy like Michael, most men don't look like him or possess that form of confidence. They have the same insecurities and emotional hang-ups as everyone else, meaning they are not drowning in a constant pool of women. They have school. They have careers. And like many of my female clients who wonder if they've focused on their ambition to the exclusion of their romantic lives, there are many men wondering the same thing. Shy, supportive but introverted men who have also been raised to think love will "just happen."

This, in some ways, creates a dating environment that favors someone like Michael in the short term. He's outgoing and tall, making himself—at least initially—attractive to a large swath of women. But his promiscuity had also put him at a disadvantage in developing the healthy relationship he craved with Lauryn.

A study by National Health and Social Life Survey in 2004 found that premarital promiscuity has a huge effect on how men conduct themselves in committed or married relationships in that the more sexual partners men have had, the less likely they were to be sensitive to their long-term partner or wife's sexual needs.

Analysts of the survey theorized that the variety in sexual activity, as well as the frequency of having emotionally unattached sex, made these once-promiscuous husbands numb to some of the bonding effects of sex between a committed couple. Sex was less special with a spouse because the man had already had so much sex and with such a variety of people that his capacity to build emotional intimacy through sex had greatly diminished. For every sexual partner, marital sexual satisfaction decreased by 5 percent for men.

Adding to this is the sexual double standard, placing conflict and guilt regarding sex from Lauryn's standpoint. Women often bear the brunt of criticism for hypersexual behavior, therefore someone like Lauryn learned to not expect much from "hookup" culture. If anything, the availability of no-strings-attached, casual sex from men in her age range had left her somewhat jaded. The initial thrill of conquest almost always gave way to feelings of shame and guilt that something was "wrong" with her. Never mind that if she had enough sex with any-one, even if she knew they weren't right for her, she would eventually grow attached, wanting more. Many studies have revealed this may have something to do with brain chemistry. During sex, for women, oxytocin is released, a bonding chemical that associ-ates the "high" sensation with whatever activity is taking place when it is released. Oxytocin plays a huge part in bonding mothers with their infants during acts such as breastfeeding. Men have a similar hormone that does the same—vasopressin—but it's been found that the more men get used to having casual sex with a variety of partners, the harder it is for them to as-sociate sex with bonding. In their book *Hooked: New Science on How Casual Sex Is Affecting Our Children,* doctors Joe McIlhaney and Freda McKissic Bush describe the overabundance of casual sex as im-pairing "[t]heir inability to bond after multiple liai-sons," describing the aftereffects as "almost like tape that loses its stickiness after being applied and re-moved multiple times."

Because she'd "bonded" in the past with men

who'd been wrong for her, Lauryn had a very real fear of being taken advantage of sexually by guys like Michael. In the past, those who'd broken her heart were good-looking, charming guys overly preoccupied with sex, who had little interest in commitment. As a young woman, it wasn't like men thought you were "awesome" for having sex with them casually, it just gained you a negative reputation for "giving" them what they wanted. Women were supposed to be the gatekeepers of sex and have scorn heaped upon them for either being too promiscuous or too chaste.

With all this in mind, at twenty-seven Lauryn put men into categories to protect her heart. Men she desired sexually but didn't think were reliable in the long-term were OK for sexual recreation but not much else, and it was important for her to cut it off before she got emotionally invested. For men she actually saw as having "potential," she often held off on sex until she felt both were equally invested emotionally in the relationship. This sometimes meant she waited a month or more to have sex. It was more about a feeling than a timetable. It was about how well they both knew each other, about conversations they'd had and time they'd spent together. It was about whether the man saw her as a person and not as a recreational sex partner.

Because Michael had so many of the traits of the men she'd been wary of since college, she never took him seriously. Michael was for sex. And when she fretted that she could potentially get attached to him emotionally if the sexual relationship without emotional commitment continued, she withdrew and put him in "the friend zone." But for someone like Michael, who expressed all emotional intimacy through sex, this was confusing. The one way he knew how to demonstrate his desire was cut off to him once Lauryn decided the relationship was going nowhere.

Our society's views of sex and gender played a huge role in why Michael saw Lauryn as "the one," but Lauryn didn't feel the same way. And these views are shaped from centuries of social conditioning, religion and gender norms. In an agrarian, pre-industrial society, women were traditionally viewed as property. A promiscuous woman was a "used" woman—not looked at much differently than a used car. A woman who wasn't virginal was viewed as being worth less than a young woman who'd never had sex. We see remnants of this today in our post–women's rights movement and the sexual revolution of the 1960s, in our "hookup" culture of college and our twenties. Like in the 2011 Anna Faris film *What's Your Number?*, where the main character becomes obsessed with searching for her "soul mate" through old boyfriends in order to keep her number of sexual partners from going up. Even in a post–sexual revolution, women are still judged for their sex—only now there's the added prejudice of a woman who is chaste being "odd" or having something wrong with her in an age when "everyone" is supposed to be "doing it," per societal pressure.

With this in mind, it's important for us to be honest about our feelings toward sex in our dating life. How we feel about sex is part of our values—no different from our beliefs in career versus family. Lauryn would have probably been surprised to learn that Michael, despite his talk of sexual experience, was actually fine with waiting to have sex with a woman. If Michael was serious about a woman, meaning he cared for her and wanted to pursue a relationship, delaying sex tended to not affect his level of interest. Michael only became frustrated with women who would have sex quickly if he never saw any relationship potential in them in the first place. But even with those women, he would often date them for months, enjoying the outings and company, because he mistook sex for love.

In turn, Michael may have been surprised to learn that Lauryn didn't put that much value on how great the sex was. While the sex had been good enough to get other women to fall hard for him, for Lauryn a combination of a man being patient and willing to learn meant more—even in terms of a sexual partner—than someone who screwed like a porn star.

If you're a good listener, if you invest in your partner's needs and emotions, chances are even a less experienced lover can learn how to please his or her partner. And that's because the desire to please is already there, in their ability to listen and adapt.

Michael, who ignored Lauryn's desire to not have a family, wasn't a good listener. He also didn't understand how important affection and non-sexual intimacy was in a relationship. Because of this, Lauryn didn't deem him a good fit for her values of a man who would be emotionally invested in her. It didn't matter that Michael was crazy about her, because she couldn't tell.

She thought Michael was just crazy about sex.

In time, Lauryn eventually found a man who could balance his sexual desire with tenderness and vulnerability. Michael, on the other hand, took a little work. Even though he and Lauryn, the dream girl, were only together for a year—thanks to his mother issues and Lauryn's perceived "perfectness"—Michael was bitter and fearful for years after the breakup.

He'd returned to his playing the field until he finally came to me and I told him to see a therapist first.

If you find yourself concerned with your relationship toward sex and intimacy, ask yourself if the following non-sexual emotional intimacies were part of your last sexual relationship.

1. I feel comfortable and relaxed outside of sex with my partner.

2. I feel my partner accepts me and values my needs and individuality.

3. My partner gives me all A's—attention, affirmation, affection and approval—whether or not sex is present.

4. My partner provides encouragement in my life and endeavors.

5. My partner is supportive when I feel sad, have a bad day or feel insecure.

The needs listed here aren't that different from what we expect from our parents, siblings or friends in order to form healthy bonds. They can apply to all sorts of situations. When these needs are met, we feel love. When they are not, we feel pain, we don't feel bonded and this leads to devaluation of the relationship, and, in some cases, ourselves. Real intimacy goes beyond sex.

CHAPTER 12

It's What They Do, Not What They Say

Your first instinct was probably right.

When he was three hours late for the first date. When she talked about her divorce for almost the entire dinner and you'd just met. When you'd dated him for a few weeks, but he seemed reluctant to ever tell you where he lived. When she wanted to move in after you only knew each other for a few weeks.

They weren't "the one."

I had a divorced client who said she ended up with her then-husband, an abusive man, because he told her, "God meant for us to be together." Now older and wiser, my client knew to be suspicious of such a statement.

"How could God say we were meant to be to-gether and not tell me," she said.

Your gut knows. Someone can say they're "fine," that their divorce is "in the past," that they're a "tra-ditionalist." I can say I'm an astronaut. But if you don't ever see me climb into a spaceship, I might be lying.

It's easy to say you're something. It's much harder to "do" or "be."

In Malcolm Gladwell's best-selling book *Blink*, he makes the case for our gut instincts, that initial feeling about something that is oh-so-often right. Af-ter all, we've been developing our gut instincts since we were babies, unconsciously reacting to some faces with a smile and to others with a scowl. We learned things like sarcasm, irony and duplicity in elementary school or when dealing with our siblings. From that game of peekaboo we finally learned you really never did disappear, we know that people aren't always what they seem. We know when things look "off." In the world of robotics and 3-D animation, the "un-canny valley" is the term used to describe when something created to look human evokes a feeling of fear or dislike. Think of your favorite animated film, then think of a film like *Final Fantasy* or *The Polar Express*, where the images are rendered to look as "human" as possible, but all the efforts to turn a se-ries of ones and zeros into faces good enough to fool a human fall short, resulting in humanlike figures that cause a sense of fear and disgust.

The harder they try, the more our brains seem to seize upon what makes these faces look inhuman.

Our gut reactions to people aren't that much different. When you sense something is "off" about your date, you've wandered into the emotional "uncanny valley"—the more this person who is wrong for you tries to convince you they're the one, the more your alarms go off.

He says he's a gentleman, but when you suggest meeting him at the coffee shop instead of riding in the car with him he takes offense and berates you for "fearing" him—even though you don't know him. Your gut says you shouldn't trust him and now it's screaming it, yet there he is attempting to pressure you into trust.

Red flag on the play. Don't ignore your gut.

The same goes for when you're on a date and you notice that the person across from you may not share your same values. Too often men and women go into relationships thinking they can change the things they don't like about their potential partners—not understanding that all too often, what you see now is what you get . . . forever.

This is why it's so important to know what you want in a relationship—what your values are, your personality and your non-starters (e.g., desire for children) in order to determine if the person you're dating shares them or has a personality complementary to your own. When we find ourselves ignoring our gut and jumping quickly into a relationship, it's typically at the expense of our values, personality and non-starters.

Why we ignore our gut often has a lot to do with the psychological act called "projection." When we see someone who fulfills our "ideal," we will often see what we want in that person who fits the type—ignoring all information to the contrary. This was definitely the case with the previous chapter's couple, Lauryn and Michael. Lauryn quickly picked up on things like Michael's maturity level and fear of intimacy as not being compatible with her personality and needs, while Michael, in his rush to make Lauryn his "dream girl," simply ignored the fact that she did not want to have kids and settle down and viewed hypersexuality as a sign of immaturity.

This projection, of seeing what we want to see, creates a sort of halo effect. We focus on our partner's looks or career or educational background to the detriment of their actual behavior or compatibility level. This is what happens when we value "type hype" over tangible needs and personality traits. Wanting a 6'2" investment banker but desiring values of unselfishness and traditionalist views on family are not mutually exclusive. You can want your type as much as you want—that doesn't mean they'll meet your needs or be good to (or for) you.

How do you know if you're projecting your desires on someone who doesn't fit your needs? Watch out for these signs:

Mirroring—In your desire for companionship do you find that you're losing yourself in the relationship—meaning, you take on his or her likes, interests, dreams, goals and even personality traits? Mirroring is where you think you will get the love you want by imitating the person you desire. But if the person you're dating can't appreciate you as an individual or you feel too insecure to talk about your needs and interests, this can open up the door for a one-sided or selfish relationship where your needs are rarely considered or met.

Rescuing—You meet your dream type, but there's a crucial value flaw—like low-self-esteem, being judgmental, an inability to be faithful or selfishness—and rather than accepting that your dream type may be flawed, you believe that through virtue of your hard work and love you can "change" them, rescuing them from themselves. The only problem with this logic is no one can make someone change or desire to be rescued—your partner has to decide that on their own. Otherwise you may find yourself trapped in a never-changing, dysfunctional relationship of constant frustration.

Auditioning—This is when you accept that your

dream guy or gal has some flaws but think that if you just are enough of a virtuous doormat, they'll finally learn to appreciate you and treat you right. It's pretty much a form of hard-core denial that confuses suffering in love with the temporary acts of "suffering for art" or "suffering for your career." It's rooted in the belief that love is supposed to be hard and that you will be rewarded if you stick it out. This makes sense if a relationship has a solid foundation in the first place, but if love is turbulent from week one, no amount of proving your relationship worthiness will fix poor behavior.

It's also important to remember that we shouldn't give our values the "type hype" treatment. Meaning, if you say you want a "traditional marriage" but you have no idea what that actually entails, or you want "a family" in an abstract sense akin to wanting a new car or a trip to Cabo, you're headed for disaster. It's not just what your relationship vitals sound like, but what they look like. What do you see when you say "monogamy"? Do you mean two people being faithful or just one person being faithful to you? And saying you value family goes beyond just a few pictures of their mother on Facebook—does this family-centered person talk about their own extended families, take time for visits, spend money on holidays and for presents during important family milestones? Are they emotionally invested in what's going on with their family? If you follow the money and how they spend their free time, you'll have a clearer picture if that vital is really a vital and not a vital mutated into "type hype."

Being obsessed with "type" causes us to try to force the love magic to happen, even though our guts tell us this won't work. Yet there we are, trying to counteract our gut, hoping against hope it's wrong. Maybe she didn't really mean it when she said she wasn't "into men"? Maybe if we just try really hard, because she's our "type," she'll come around and stop being a lesbian.

Maybe. But I doubt it. There's not much you can do in the way of mirroring, rescuing, auditioning or projecting that can counteract our natural urges and personalities.

Why we get obsessed with the types we find attractive is often rooted in our families. Back to Lauryn and Michael—Lauryn was distrustful of men (and the institution of marriage) because of how her father behaved in her parents' divorce. He was cold, removed himself from her life completely in an effort to get back at his wife, refused to pay child support and constantly let her down—promising trips to the zoo or shopping sprees for holidays or good grades that never took place. Lauryn learned at an early age from the first man she ever loved that a man's love could not be trusted.

This bled into many of her adult dating relationships where she, as a much younger woman, sometimes tolerated abusive and cruel behavior, thinking
"all" men were like her father. By the time she met
Michael, she'd been in therapy for a few years and
realized her issue was with her father, not so much
the lousy college hookups of her youth. Still, it was
hard for her to trust, so she moved slowly in giving
up her heart.

Michael had mother issues. Even though he had
a "loving" relationship with his mom, that initial
abandonment had fostered a fear in him that he
found difficult to overcome. Whenever he met a
woman he felt strongly about, it triggered that fear of
being left behind, causing him to not want to emotionally invest in the relationship—even if he thought
the woman was the "perfect girl."

Although these issues are easy to spot after a
partner tells you, for most of us, we only get a hint of
the familial damage that has been inflicted upon
those on the dating battlefield. We have to do a lot of
gut-guesswork, meaning that in the case of a couple
like Michael and Lauryn, they dated for a year before
Lauryn realized there wasn't a future.

Typically, if you've dated and/or are engaged to
marry someone for about two years and no move has
been made toward greater commitment, marriage is
unlikely to happen. In two years' time, three years at

the most, many of us know if our guts are faulty in any way, and if you've reached the two-year point in a relationship—and your goal is marriage—you need to make a serious assessment as to whether it's worth sticking it out. Because if you're certain of marriage and the other party isn't, that means their gut doesn't feel so hot about you.

And if their gut isn't nudging you toward "the one" status, it never will.

Over time in any relationship, the familiarity should be creating bonds, fostering better emotional security and self-esteem, and you should be healthily negotiating the terms of your commitment. If in two or three years one partner is still emotionally distant, if you're still projecting your desires while finding yourself changing or hoping your partner changes, if you feel even more emotionally insecure than when the relationship began—chances are that even if you do get married, your relationship is going to be fraught with the same problems that plagued it while you were dating.

How many times have you known someone or you, yourself, found that you spent years waiting for a relationship to end in marriage only to have it end and for your partner to quickly move on—even, in some cases, to marry someone else?

Too often, and I've found this more with women I have counseled than men, there is a tendency to invest in a relationship that they hope will turn into marriage—even if there are obvious signs of problems. Often they seemed to be in emotionally unfulfilling relationships with men who are uncertain about their future or have already repeatedly stated they were not interested in a long-term commitment with them. Yet these women invest years, often even moving in with their partners, believing these steps will lead to marriage.

They find themselves acting out those projector roles of mirroring, rescuing and auditioning, thinking there is some set of behaviors that will turn a flawed relationship into marriage. And often the commitment-phobic men aren't so much afraid of commitment but are listening to their gut—they know the relationship will not work in the long-term—while still enjoying all the creature comforts that come with having a significant other.

Naturally, there are exceptions to this; you will find men willing to overinvest in a relationship that is going nowhere fast, but women are often bombarded with more messages that a man can be "changed." It shows up in our fiction constantly. Take the Disney version of *The Little Mermaid*, which puts a happy ending on a fairy tale that's actually about the price you pay when you give up too much for love. Instead of a wedding, the titular mermaid in Hans Christian Andersen's story ends up dead, turning into sea foam. Women, again due to years of social conditioning where their happiness depended greatly on getting married, are bombarded with messages to temper their expectations with men, settle for less and believe that bad behavior is something that can be corrected through the virtuous power of love. That's a hard pathology to override when the narrative was created to justify a woman's suffering in a bad marriage.

Because of this, so many women I've counseled have stayed in relationships that were doomed from the beginning—because they didn't pay attention to what their partners did. They only saw what they wanted to see. Ignoring the "he will never marry you" elephant in the room.

This is why it's so important to judge a partner's behaviors. Do they take consideration of your needs? Do they share your values? Are your personalities comparable? Are they emotionally supportive? Are they affectionate? Are they reliable? Do you both want commitment? Are they willing to open up their hearts and lives to you? These are the things you should be studying and judging. These are the things that will tell your gut you have made the right choice.

When there is insecurity in what should be a non-problematic part of a relationship, that is what your gut is picking up on. Trust it.

It may feel like you have a feeling, but are you watching all the telltale signs that they may be into you?

- Do they self-groom while talking to you? Like touch their hair or straighten their tie? Do they subconsciously pull on their pants, shirt or skirt? That means they're thinking of how they look and how they want to look good—for you.

- Belly button pointed toward you? Good.

- Legs, knees pointed toward you? Even better.

- Do they cross their legs toward you on top of all that? They're really paying attention and their body is an arrow pointing to you.

- When you smile, do they smile? When you laugh, do they laugh? When you touch yourself on your knee, neck, arm or torso, do they touch themselves as well? They're mirroring, which is a sign of both interest and flattery.

- Do they mimic your speech? I'm not talking about mocking your accent, but do they subconsciously start using your turns of phrase, idioms, slang or speech patterns? They're trying to get to know you and are really paying close attention—albeit subconsciously.

- Do they touch your arm or hand while talking? Excellent sign if they're looking for a polite way to invade your space and get closer.

- Do they touch their lips, collarbone or face in a caressing or interesting way? They may be subconsciously wishing it was you touching them. Especially if they're smiling and nodding with their belly button pointed toward you when they're doing it.

Remember, if someone looks or sounds into you, trust your gut. They probably are and it's worth the risk.

CHAPTER 13

Dating Is a Numbers Game

Love is like the lotto—you have to play to win.

Never has it been more important to let go of this notion that love "just happens." Nothing just happens. Your education didn't "just happen." The friends you sought out and made didn't "just happen." Your career, your lifestyle, your talents, your hobbies and interests—none of those things "just happened." You personally invested. You were down for trial. Prepared for error, then ready to try again.

Finding a husband or wife doesn't "just happen" for most people. Sure, there are those rare few who trip and fall into their perfect romance, but you also might get plucked out of obscurity by an acting scout and become a Hollywood star. Most actors making million-dollar paydays in summer blockbusters were kicking around the business for years, putting in hours working and networking, hustling and honing their craft. There are very few true "overnight" celebrities. The same goes for that kismet meeting that sets it all in motion.

I have a friend whose parents met when her mother came to her father's apartment one day with a mutual friend of theirs. And while he found his future wife by happy accident, it wasn't an accident for her. In her efforts to find a spouse, she'd networked with friends and coworkers, which their mutual friend was, and he introduced them. It "just happened" for my friend's father, but it was her mother who made it happen by getting out there.

She had to kiss a lot of frogs before she met her prince.

So will you.

Because dating is a numbers game.

Twenty-four men and $3,000. That's how many men a survey of women in the United Kingdom had to go out with on average before they found "the one." And that's how much money those women had to spend on styling, dressing and socializing to get to their guy.

According to the dating site eHarmony half of all singles in the United States haven't been on one date in the past two years. This means that a lot of people who should be playing are sitting out of the dating game on the sidelines. That means 80 percent of all dating is done by only 20 percent of single people. We simply don't date as frequently as we need to find love, but we spend a lot of time hooking up and hanging out—which, sorry, isn't dating.

What's a date? It's strange that I even have to ask that question, but don't be surprised by how many people aren't sure. A date—or the act of dating—is when two people agree to participate in mutual "getting to know you" activities (not including sex) over a period of time. A date is when you make a plan to meet somewhere to go do something together (again, that doesn't involve sex) and you have that experience, spend that time and find out if there's a bond.

Dates are crucial if your goal is finding a husband or wife.

A study done by UKDating.com found that 7 percent of the more than two thousand women they surveyed went on forty-one to sixty dates before they found a husband. One percent had to go on sixty-one to eighty dates. But no matter what, there was one true thing for every woman in that survey—she had to keep going out and keep getting dates until she found the guy. The minute you take yourself out of the game, you have given up the number one proactive thing you can do to find love and have left it up to the fates of the cosmos.

Maybe Jesus will take the wheel in your love life. But just maybe he's expecting you to get out there and go out on some dates.

Many of my clients, especially the female ones, were not dating enough when they first sought me out. Some hadn't gone on dates in years, others months.

First of all—how is he ever going to meet you (or you meet him), if you're not out there? And before you point out to me that you're not turning down dates left and right from men or women tripping over themselves to get to you, it doesn't work that way. Waiting for someone to approach you or waiting for the dating opportunity to happen, rather than creating situations where you can meet people to date, is a passive approach. Dating only works if you work the dating field like you work your career dreams and business ambitions—apply to your dating life the same dedication, self-starter attitude and curiosity you take to work every day for the best results.

Treat dating like an entrepreneurial venture. Like an ambitious new career. Like the quest for your dream job. Are you up for it?

Assessment: If you're about to enter the dating market, you need to self-assess. Are you ready to start seriously dating? If so, are you prepared to do what it takes to be the best version of youself when you head out looking for people to date? This means thinking about how you dress, your hair, personal hygiene and grooming habits, how you speak and introduce yourself, your self-esteem and confidence levels, your level of comfort when talking to strangers. Think about yourself critically—would you date you?

Make a list: Outline which qualities you feel are your strengths in your effort to get dates and make an additional list of the things you perceive as weaknesses.

Develop a strategy: Of the good qualities—how can you enhance them? How can you make them stand out more and work for you? For instance, are you good at talking (even though you might be only so-so at flirting)? That's something you can build on. The gift of gab helps draw people in. Loquaciousness hints at your charisma potential. Put yourself in more situations where you can actually have conversations with new people where the impetus isn't so much "hooking up." Meaning, as a conversationalist, the club—with the loudness—is a weak spot for you. But a social or networking mixer, a book club, a charity event or any activity where striking up a conversation is not just easy but expected? That's the ticket. Of your characteristics that you consider negatives, how can you best transform them into positives? Feel like you've put on some weight? Get more into both fitness and fashion. I can't stress enough the importance of buying clothes that actually fit. Fashion doesn't come naturally to everyone, but it's worth the investment if you're dating to have a wardrobe that fits well and flatters the figure. Looking your best will boost your own self-esteem and you may find your weight wasn't so much the issue, but how you were dressing yourself was. A thin guy wearing too-large clothes might look sloppy to prospective dates. A pear-shaped woman wearing an empire-waist or sack-style dress might be accidentally making herself look larger than she actually is. When we wear clothes that flatter us and our shapes, we're dressing for dating success.

Be a student: It's never too late to learn how to be the best you can possibly be. Because you might not have dated in a while, it might be time to do a little brush up. A little practice makes perfect. Find low-stress public situations where you can practice introducing yourself to others, remembering names and having first conversations. Study your posture and practice how you speak in a mirror. Naturally, many of us have never actually seen ourselves speak. Have a friend record you talking while standing so you can notice what you do (or don't do) with your hands. Do you stand up straight? Study your own body language and the body language of others so you get better at picking up on signals of interest and disinterest. Then get out there, with good old trial and error, learning from your results. Don't become devastated when you mess up or someone politely declines your overture; just get right back out there and try to learn from/correct whatever mistakes you think you may have made. The only way to get good at dating, flirting, talking and meeting new people is to do it.

Get out there (and not just to a club): R & B singer Usher Raymond once sang of finding "Love in This Club," and for some folks, maybe you can. But let's not put all our romantic eggs in the discotheque basket. The best way to meet new people is to do something different, even challenging, from what you would normally do to force you out of your element and get you to interact with others. This means that when you go out with the intention of meeting people you either go out alone or only with one other person—and you split up with that person when you get to the place so you can mingle. This means taking on activities—not just the bar scene—like day hikes, dance lessons, art gallery openings, conferences and trade conventions, martial arts classes, charity/volunteer work, book signings, boxing lessons, joining an amateur sporting league and outdoor city events, such as open markets, street fairs, carnivals, festivals, cookouts and other social gatherings. The more atypical the activity from what you'd normally do, the better. With new things, you'll be more apt to meet new people from outside of your typical social circle. If there's something you've always wanted to try out, now is the time to do it—all under the guise that you have to get out there anyway. You're looking for dates.

Work your networks: Online dating, social networking and your friends and family are all great outlets for meeting new people—and potential dates. A great dating profile online—even a well-maintained Facebook page—can create dating opportunities. It also doesn't hurt to let those who care about you the most know you're out there looking. You never know who may know who.

Get around: For some people it might sound odd that I recommend dating more than one person at a time. This isn't about turning men and women into "players" but maximizing your options by taking advantage of as many of those options as possible. It's about the "Paradox of Choice," a bit of psychological theorizing that presupposes that when people are faced with having to choose one option out of many desirable choices, they will begin to consider hypothetical trade-offs. Sometimes this leads to options being evaluated in terms of missed opportunities instead of the potential of an opportunity, but I believe this actually works in your favor in dating multiple people as you search for a partner. We need to have options when dating because finding someone should not be about someone's "potential" as a mate. Focus on who actually stands before you in the present.

Don't fall in love with "potential." Fall for what's substantial and real and in your hands to choose from.

Now, doing these things—like becoming really focused on your body language, grooming and hitting up new places—isn't about being "thirsty." It isn't that you've been wandering in the desert of loneliness and now you are scavenging for whatever you can find. Desperation isn't hot. Ever. This is about being smart and creating opportunity.

Once you've gotten out there and you've gotten the dates, now is the time to follow through. Schedule initial quick dates for coffee so you can better get to know each other.

I know, you're like, "This coffee thing again?"

Yes, the coffee thing! It works. Believe me. It's safe because it's public. It's low pressure because it's laid-back and communal. It's quiet enough for conversation. It's economical (a small cup of plain coffee is still under the three-dollar price point at most places). And, because of all that caffeine, kind of arousing. Coffee gives you a buzz and makes you alert, makes you pay more attention. And you're going to need to do a lot of that on your coffee date so you can better determine when it's time to move from the java hut to something more serious.

When it comes time to plan the real date, really listen to your potential partner, learn what they like and don't like, what their interests and hobbies are, then try to find innovative ways to incorporate them. If they're very touchy-feely, take them dancing. If they like gifts, take them to a painting class and surprise them at the end by giving them the painting. Also, don't be afraid to suggest an activity that's new to the both of you. Often the best way to learn about yourself and the person you're dating is to launch yourselves into uncharted waters. New challenges open up new emotions, energies and conversation starters—and they definitely make the date memorable.

Once you get out there, meeting and mixing it up, it's important to remember to play fair. Respect those you date as you'd want to be respected. That means being truthful, and giving full disclosure of your intentions. If you just want to go out and have fun and you are seeing other people—that should be cleared up fairly early on.

Most important, though, have fun! Remember my client who I told to have ten dates over thirty days? She ended up going on fifty-two dates in less than three months! Take your own version of my dating challenge, but if you're still working on things, give yourself sixty days to have ten dates. The only way to find "the one" is to get out there, and you can't get out there if you don't get moving. Make a pact with yourself that this year is the year you're coming out of your shell. This year you will date and you'll have fun.

Not all date spots are created equal!

GOOD: An interstate commuter train trip. Nothing like taking the Acela train from Washington, D.C., to New York City and finding love along the route— or racing up to the city via train for a fun day-date.

BAD: The club. It's loud. It's crowded. It's oddly impersonal even though someone is sweating on you. Bad idea, buddy.

GOOD: Going out with just one friend and splitting up so you can both mingle and meet people.

BAD: Going on a date with a group of friends. How can you get to know a new person with all your old people around judging every move? And how do you have a one-on-one convo?

GOOD: Hitting the gym. Physical activities can get the blood pumping and the heart racing in more ways than one. Plus, gyms are great places to meet people. More adventurous fitness classes like a new type of yoga or aggressive spin class might be a good place for you and a date to test your stamina.

BAD: An overnight first date. You don't know each other well enough to spend *that* much time together yet. Keep that first date around two hours, maybe three. Let's not go there all night. Not yet.

GOOD: Hit up an annual event—like a holiday party or county fair. Where there are people, there are potential dates to find. And imagine how much you could learn about your potential partner on a first date checking out a nostalgia-filled, old-fashioned traveling carnival?

BAD: Movies. How can you get to know each other and talk when you're both watching Robert Downey Jr.'s *Iron Man*?

CHAPTER 14

Your Friends Are Not
Relationship Experts

Kelly's friends really meant well. They honestly did. Especially Marla. Twice-divorced, bitter Marla, whose father walked out on her mother when she was eleven, never to be heard from again, whose brother was in prison and who believed all men cheat, no man could be trusted, that most of them weren't worth the trouble, and that of course Kelly was single, because all the "good" men were dead, married or gay.

Marla's dating advice usually boiled down to—don't. But if you do? Don't trust anyone. Which would make perfect sense if your life was heavily impacted by largely negative experiences with men. But Kelly was only twenty-five, never married, a college grad and had a good relationship with her father, even after her parents were divorced. Yet it was easy to fall into Marla's bitterness trap because it wasn't like she was making up her bad experiences with men. All those things did happen to her. But just because your friend went to the moon the other day, it doesn't make all of us astronauts.

Our personal life experiences that shape us are just that—they're our personal life experiences, all colored and tailored specifically for ourselves. Just because you can eat Thai food without going into shock and almost dying doesn't mean you should order pad thai for your friend with the severe nut allergy. What was true for Marla wasn't true for Kelly.

The same goes for Michael, the emotionally distant Romeo from chapter 11, whose friends were too busy high-fiving his sexual prowess to notice Michael's newfound desire for women and to take him seriously. Especially his male friends who either regretted their marriages or were recently divorced and were living vicariously through him. In their frustration they couldn't see why Michael wanted to get serious with any woman. They encouraged him to put anything and everything ahead of whomever he was dating, no matter how he felt about her. In their advice they all talked in stereotypes—all women want is money, all pretty women are shallow, all career women are controlling or distant, etc.

Again, their advice was colored by their own jaded experiences. While they were good to blow off steam with or to throw around some half-thought-out insight, these weren't the best people to take advice from. Their bias was far too high for any kind of objectivity.

Your friends are your friends. Funny, thoughtful, dependable and supportive. But they aren't therapists. They aren't dating experts. And as the old saying goes, opinions are like assholes—everyone has one.

Consider the source.

Your loved ones often give bad advice. Well-meaning but awful dating advice. Because they aren't objective. Will your friends actually tell you that you don't know how to dress and have a hygiene issue . . . or will they say that a woman should just "accept you for you"? Will your friends tell you that you were overreacting when twelve hours had passed since the initial meeting and he still hadn't texted you back . . . or will they encourage whatever half-baked theory has developed in your panicking mind? Our friends want to believe in us and support us and protect us, which means sometimes their advice is more about boosting our own self-esteem or validating us as a friend—instead of giving us valuable criticism we can apply to change our dating fortune.

Even our parents can give some suspect advice. It's natural to want to consult your mom and dad, as these are typically the same people who taught you how to use the restroom and read. There was a point in your young life where you thought they were both superhuman geniuses simply because they could reach above the counter and make food. So there's this tendency to take our parents' advice wholesale without also questioning their credibility and/or motivations. Our parents have the potential to be just as biased and flawed in their views as our friends, but with the added pressure of being your parents, with all complexities, complexes and problems that come with them.

When the parent/child relationship is somewhat conflicted—like perhaps your mother is domineering and controlling, or your father is bitter or conflicted—we can fall into this trap of thinking we can't change our relationship with them, or our futures, as we believe what happened to them will happen to us. Kelly's friend Marla felt her man-based disappointment was unavoidable because of how her father was, therefore she didn't stop herself from repeating her mother's mistakes. If something is "inevitable" you will spend your time waiting for the tragedy to strike—not enjoying the relationship. Meaning, if you were the type of man who was even-tempered, reliable and faithful, Marla spent a lot of time being completely paranoid about you, waiting for you to finally "fail." When a relationship turned out to be dysfunctional she was almost happy, as it was a validation of her worldview. She knew how to handle a cruel and unreliable man.

A good one? What was that? Marla didn't know what to do with that. Therefore she decided he didn't exist.

There is a prevailing thought that if a woman has a bad relationship with her father, or a man has a bad relationship with his mother, they will have destructive, psychologically conflicted relationships with the opposite sex. Legendary psychoanalysts Sigmund Freud and Carl Jung developed theories, calling them Oedipal and Electra complexes, respectively, to describe our conflicted relationships with our parents. In short, the Oedipus complex is a male's unconscious desire to sexually possess his mother and kill his father, and the Electra complex is a female's unconscious competition with her mother and desire to sexually possess her father. And while those two terms—and Freud's and Jung's conclusions—are heavily debated, controversial even, there is a lot of research to back that our relationships with our parents affect our dating life. Especially in that we often, subconsciously, find ourselves trying to work out our parent/child relationships in our relationships with friends and lovers.

Dr. Meg Meeker, author of *Strong Fathers, Strong Daughters: 10 Secrets Every Father Should*

Know, talks quite a bit about how a girl's first experience of love is with her father, hence coloring her future views of all male/female relationships.

In an interview with talk show host Oprah Winfrey for Oprah's radio show on SiriusXM, Dr. Meeker said: "If there is positive male experience in her early years, she is going to do much better. If she has a bad experience when she is young, she is going to be very put off by all male figures in her life. That's the power of a dad."

On the mother/son end, author Michael Gurian penned *The Invisible Presence*, a book that examines how a boy's interactions with his mother affect his most intimate relationships. Gurian writes: "[I]t is about the son's claiming and reclaiming of his own female side, the femaleness and that femininity which, as psychologist Herb Goldberg has put it, 'is a part of every man's core.'"

Men with troubled relationships with their mothers sometimes have stressful relationships with women, marked by concerns and fears about control. Some men with overbearing mothers may be both overly dependent on their partners, yet at the same time resentful if the partner is assertive or potentially domineering.

But according to both Gurian and Dr. Meeker, none of us have to be bound to our upbringing. Believing that all your relationships will be conflicted because your first relationship with your parents was is akin to believing that if you're born poor you'll die that way, as well. There are steps you can take to get out of poverty and to create a better life for yourself.

There are also steps you can take to overcome a harsh emotional past. Our relationship with our parents isn't absolute. We can move forward, get clarity, get closure and gain control. A bad primary experience as a child doesn't have to trump all future experiences. With hard work you can overwrite the bad tape in your head telling you to always expect the worst. You can find objectivity and learn from your more troublesome relationships so you can avoid that pain repeating itself, while also being open to meeting someone new and trying again.

Dr. Meeker told Oprah, "My great hope is that even if there is some terrible damage that is passed between a daughter and a dad, it's never too late to correct it."

We aren't victims of our circumstances. We can find control.

And it starts right here.

Declare your own emotional independence—and get your friends and family out of your dating life. Your search for finding who is best for you is a solo journey that eventually becomes a twosome when you find your potential significant other. There's no room for a busload of people you aren't dating, piling on their baggage and past conflicts.

Here's how to start:

- **Create a "no-prying" policy:** If you want to talk about your relationships you will tell them what you feel comfortable revealing. Friends and family don't need a running monologue.

- **Set boundaries:** A good rule in general for any relationship, in the case of your family and friends, is to make it clear that you make your own decisions and you choose who is (and isn't) in your life. You want to both give and receive respect. If there's no mutual respect, it's unlikely your mother or father will respect dating decisions independent of their thoughts.

- **No need for introductions:** Ideally, if you're doing the dating challenge right, you're going to go out with a lot of people. Your friends and families don't need to meet any of those people unless the relationship has taken a turn for the very serious. By introducing a potential suitor too soon you invite attention, criticism and comments on someone you're still just getting to know. Their insight isn't of much use when you don't know much more than they do about who you're going out with.

Sometimes, though, even setting these guidelines isn't enough if the relationship you have with a friend or relative is toxic. In that case, it might be time to cut the proverbial cord and walk away.

This means letting go of expecting much from friends and family who (a) feel like you must always need them or are unnecessarily needy of you, (b) who feel they don't deserve healthy, balanced relationships and (c) are stuck emotionally, such as always angry or fixated on some past trauma.

Along with the aforementioned establishment of good, healthy boundaries, to end these problematic relationships you should:

- Decrease the time spent with the problematic friend or relative.

- Address the importance of attending to your own needs and the needs of others who are not your toxic friend/relative.

- Take a break or a sabbatical from the relationship to see if some time apart will do you both some good.

- In worst-case scenarios, where the relationship has become unnecessarily controlling or even abusive, it might be best to cut them out of your life.

It's important to not feel guilty for having to do what we must to protect ourselves and stay emotionally healthy. Not everyone you love deserves to be in your life if they're hurting you. You have the right to be happy and to be free from the dysfunction and pain of past relationships. You have the control. You can change it.

Now, because there are no hard and fast rules in interpersonal communications, it's important to remember that in our quest to make good decisions about dating, not all advice is bad. All advice is simply suspect until you determine the veracity of the source and/or determine whether the advice fits your situation. This is why knowing the source is so important. Someone who has successful relationships and presents you with (a) real facts (not just passionate opinion) and (b) tangible steps you can take probably has some decent advice to give.

But that "good" advice still has to fit you. Which is why many of us are drawn to the professionals.

Obviously, you weren't too afraid to go to a professional, as you're—right now—reading this book.

And there are a lot of people whose life's work involves helping people get along better with one another and find the love they want. But they're not all equal and some are better for more situations than others. The "love industry" isn't that much different from the medical industry—you can go to a general practitioner or a specialist, but you have to seek help from the professional who fits best. You wouldn't go to a neurologist for your flu; you don't seek a psychiatrist to help you with your asthma. Different love professionals do very specific things.

Here's a quick guide:

Therapists/psychologists: Wonderful if you've determined that the number one barrier between you and love is your own emotional hang-ups. If you think your love life is dysfunctional due to your past relationships, your parents or a mental health issue, these individuals are the best to get you on the path of self-love and acceptance—a crucial path for those seeking healthy love.

Life coaches: While a therapist often speaks in the abstract and works as an objective observer in your life, life coaches take an assessment of who you are, your personality and your troubles and then tell you what steps you can take to solve your problems. They help clients develop plans to get them out of a rut and out into the world. They're great if you find your dating woes are more about motivation and needing some direction than some emotionally crippling psychosis.

Matchmakers: These are the folks you call when you're serious about going out on dates and finding a spouse—as that is all they do. Matchmakers are like the real estate agents of romance—we get you staged for matrimony like agents get a house staged for sale. We help correct bad habits or behaviors that may be keeping you from attracting those you desire, get you in the marriage mind-set and get you out there, meeting people, going on dates and making connections.

Body language experts: Everyone should talk to a body language expert at some point, if only to learn a bit more about themselves and how they may be coming across to the world. A body language expert will be able to pick up your bad body habits that make you seem intimidating when you want to appear inviting, make you look insecure when you're actually quite assertive and successful. They'll have you standing up straight, speaking clearly and looking confident in no time.

And again, even with these love professionals, remember—know your source.

Research the love doctor you're reaching out to, ask for testimonials, talk to previous clients, research their background. Many of these services don't come cheap and even an expert can be flawed. Shop around, have preliminary visits, interviews and conversations to feel out the treatment and the specialist.

Get to know them before you go to them and commit to their services. You're the one with the control and the only one who will truly know if their advice is right for you.

Trust your gut and get out there.

You just met someone new and mentioned it to someone close to you, but did their reaction sound like they just took a bite out of the "Bitter Lover Lemon"? Maybe it's because past experience has them seeing all love as sour. Here are some people you should always take love advice from with a grain of salt:

- **The recently divorced:** Of course they grunted when you said you were dating again. As far as they're concerned, they just got out of love jail and are trying to save you from getting locked in there.

- **The settler:** Instead of waiting for Mr. or Mrs. Right, they married the person of Right Now and have lived to regret it. Much like the recently divorced, they think they're saving you from yourself.

- **Your ex–significant other:** Sure, you're still friends, but didn't you break up with them for a reason?

- **The wandering eye:** The opposite of the settler, they'll never let anyone tie them down. They think love is best by the bounty and think monogamy goes against their biological imperatives.

- **The recently burned:** They once dated one or two wandering eyes, or maybe three. Or maybe several. Now the only eyes they see are the kinds who stray—whether they're real or imagined.

- **The judge:** This is someone in your life who isn't very objective when it comes to you. They overexamine every relationship you have, bring up your past, criticize your current paramour and almost always tell you to prepare for the worst—even on your wedding day.

When dealing with the negative nellies of your family and friends, remember—they don't have to know everything about who you date, where you go and what you do. Create some emotional distance.

CHAPTER 15

Communication and Conflict Resolution Are Key

The four most feared words in a relationship: "We need to talk."

It's scary when your mother says it. You fret about being reprimanded or fired when your boss says it. And if the person you're romantically involved with says it, you're likely fraught with nervousness and fear.

"Talk about what," you think. "What did I do now?"

We always dread hearing criticism or bad news or learning that we may have hurt someone. But it's not the "we need to talk" that hurts relationships—it's when you didn't do enough talking leading up to those four dreaded words, causing them to rear their ugly heads.

Some of us will do anything to avoid "the talk." Not idle talk or shoptalk or happy talk but serious, relationship-building, hopes/dreams/fears/concerns talk. The kind of talk that tells you whether someone is an acquaintance or a close friend. The kind of talk where secrets are shared, you go deep into your needs and desires—you get real.

And some of us just don't like getting real.

But we like relationships, so we try to compensate in other ways. Some people focus more on being a good provider. Others work on their looks and personal style. I've known a few folks who thought any problem could be solved by just having sex. Some would rather bake you a cake or buy you jewelry or surprise you with flowers than say, "I'm sorry."

But you know what? You still need to say, "I'm sorry."

Strangely, avoiding talking doesn't solve the problem of "we need to talk."

Talking does.

There's this saying that when all you have is a hammer, every problem looks like a nail. The same applies to dating when you have a limited skill set. So what if you're good-looking, successful, funny, smart or wealthy? None of that is an indicator of whether your relationship will last ten years or ten days.

But you know what is? Your capacity for endless negotiation.

All relationships—whether romantic or platonic—are moored in communication and conflict resolution. They're the pillars. The better you are at communicating your wants and needs in an effective, persuasive and understanding manner, the more likely your wants and needs will not be neglected in the relationship. The better you are at solving a problem or reaching a negotiated solution, the more likely your relationships will go the distance.

If you want relationship harmony it's very important to hone your skills in those areas, starting with closing your mouth and opening your eyes and ears.

If you can't listen, you can't love: That sounds harsh, but if your ideal love is one that always wants what you want and never has a cross word to say, then your ideal love is an inhuman android or a vegetable. A relationship is not supposed to be a running monologue. Take a deep breath, pause and actually listen to what your partner has to say.

Take a long look: Words say so much, but your partner's body says a lot more. Being able to read those unspoken cues will portend the difference between your partner saying she's "fine" as in "OK," versus "fine" as in "silently seething with contempt." Obviously, one of those is a bit more crucial to your relationship longevity than the other.

Don't assume: The only person you can speak for in a relationship is yourself. You know how you feel. You only think you know how your partner feels. Never simply assume they will like/dislike, love/hate, want/not want something because you think they would. No matter how well you know them, no one wants to have their input unwanted and left out of the conversation. Make a decision with your partner together where you always take into account how they think and feel—by not assuming you know how they think or feel.

Make time for talk: Fifteen minutes in the morning. A conversation while cooking and eating dinner together. A thirty-minute call during a lunch break. While it's a nice notion that conversations will happen spontaneously, in our busy lives we often have to make time for conversation. Schedule it if you have to so you and your partner stay on the same page.

Stop the distractions: TV time is TV time and talk time is the time when you turn off the TV (and its cousins, the laptop and smartphone) and you talk. It's the same reason why sleep specialists tell those who suffer from insomnia to not keep a TV in their bedroom and to not do work in bed. Just as in sleep therapy you must establish that the bedroom is for sleeping and stage the room to that dozy effect, talk time between yourself and your partner can't get drowned out in frenzied multitasking.

Once you get the conversation going, remember, all this talk has to follow up with good conflict resolution skills. You need to be a problem solver, a good negotiator. Once issues arise, you need to be able to helpfully and fairly hash them out.

You start by establishing what the issues are, outlining the potential solutions, negotiating those solutions, then considering outside help when necessary. And that outside help sometimes may come in the form of individual or couples counseling.

Counseling is an important step in conflict resolution, especially if one or both parties feels there's an imbalance in the relationship due to misunderstanding, unfairness or long-standing issues you two have discussed but have not found a resolution for. A counselor is an outside voice who isn't for or against either of you, but is looking to give objective assessments and to mediate both sides toward a healthy conclusion. Too often couples reach out to therapists or counselors after the relationship has already taken a hard turn for the worst, usually as a last-ditch measure. But therapy is much more effective when both sides are still very committed to the relationship and are still open to change and new ideas. Often when we wait too long, after our hearts and minds have hardened, the counseling only points to the "resolution" of a couple breaking up.

There are also other barriers. Many men don't

feel comfortable asking for outside help in a relationship—often because in American culture they are raised to think that needing help or expressing any feeling outside of anger is inappropriate. But this inability to express other emotions in healthy ways, have an outlet for addressing issues with their partners or seeking the help of a professional, hurts men greatly—both in terms of their personal health and the emotional health of their relationships.

Again, even if you've been raised to never discuss your pain or feelings, there is no way to get out of the "we need to talk" scenario without talking. Couples therapy can help a partner who's not as adept at communication express him- or herself in a safe, helpful environment. And going to a counselor isn't a sign of emotional failure. Any long-term relationship will enter periods of conflict. Having an impartial, objective party to hear both sides of an issue can be very useful in resolving ongoing issues with fairness and understanding.

Counselors are most effective if:

- You fight your way through your problems, looking for winners and losers in your personal conflicts, rather than talking, listening and negotiating with each other.

- You're struggling with issues involving those outside of the relationship affecting the relationship, i.e., friends, in-laws, exes, children, etc.

- You have unresolved debates over child-rearing.

- You have stopped talking to each other or one partner has become emotionally distant.

- There are difficulties surrounding sex.

- There are problems with cheating, lying or trust.

In our effort to better understand ourselves and those we love, we have to do the emotional heavy lifting. There's no avoiding it. If you want someone to give you their heart and share their life with you, for a healthy relationship, you have to be willing to do the same. You have to know how to make things right when you know you have wronged. You have to harness the power of "I'm sorry," "I love you" and forgiveness.

Once you have decided to dedicate yourself to someone, you have to accept that problems will arise, you or your partner will make mistakes; but if you're in it for the long haul, you have to find resolutions to your problems that work for the both of you. You have to communicate and you have to be willing to be vulnerable in that communication.

When you have wronged someone or someone has wronged you, it's fine to get angry. Being able to declare your love, talk out your feelings and move toward forgiveness does not mean you never get upset. It's fine to be angry and express that anger in a responsible and healthy manner. In fact, if you don't allow your own or your partner's anger to take place it hinders the path to forgiveness. But anger can't lead to revenge or one-upmanship. It can't devolve into a cycle of retaliatory strikes and psychological warfare. If the goal is to preserve and strengthen the relationship, those who cause pain need to be able to make amends, apologize and do the work of winning back trust, and those who are the victims must find a way to forgive and work through that process with their partner.

To start that process, you must:

1. Isolate what the actual problem is.

2. Address the feelings associated with this problem directly and honestly.

3. Turn feelings of hurt or anger into language and have a substantive conversation—not a rage-induced rant or diatribe.

4. Apologize, followed by acceptance of the apology.

5. Begin the process of forgiveness.

In love, you get what you give, and you give out what you get. If the relationship is uneven, where all the emotional burdens of communication and conflict resolution weigh heavily on one partner, you may find the relationship failing, as the more emotionally burdened half grows to resent being the sole one to mentally and emotionally invest in the long-term relationship. We can't avoid "we need to talk" if we want to keep our love. We can't be afraid of our feelings or of confronting them.

The path to relationship success is through greater understanding. And greater understanding leads to a greater, more patient and stronger love.

After a fight, once the dust has settled, it's time to formulate a strategy for moving on. But are you ready to go there or just gearing up for round two? Ask yourself these questions:

- Were my needs and concerns clearly addressed?

- Was there a point reached of mutual understanding?

- Was there an apology given and accepted on either side?

- Is the conclusion both sides came to a fair compromise that takes into account all views, feelings and burdens?

- Can I live with the conclusion to this discussion?

- Can I move past it without revisiting and expecting that in revisiting I will receive a different or more favorable resolution?

It's important when we have disagreements to deal with them quickly, never letting them linger. As problems arise, address them either right away or after some preliminary thought on the best way to present yourself and your concerns. Write them down if necessary, so that your partner can clearly see where you're coming from.

CHAPTER 16

Those Aren't Your Kids

Twenty-six percent of American households are single-parent households, meaning there's a good chance the person you date may have a child of their own. If you can't deal with this, be honest, but if you think you can, remember, the kid's needs are always number one.

And no matter how much you like that kid, unless you're married and you adopt little him or her—that's not your kid.

First off, if you're dating and you're thirty or older, you may have to accept the fact that quite a few of your peers already have children. While U.S. Census data has shown that we're getting married later and later, from getting hitched out of high school to now first marriages averaging around the mid- to late twenties for both men and women—not everyone is delaying having kids. And it's not because there's a surge in unwanted teen pregnancies—those have actually gone down in recent years. A recent survey by the Centers for Disease Control and Prevention found that for girls between the ages of fifteen and nineteen, 57 percent of them had never had sex, up from a rate of 49 percent in 1995. Nowadays the face of unplanned pregnancy is actually an adult woman who already has some general idea of how she would end up with a child.

People may delay marriage, but they don't forsake having sex, or children. With every sexual encounter, even if you utilized preventive measures, there's always a chance you could get pregnant. The condom breaks, you forget to take your birth control pills and next thing you know—baby. According to the National Campaign to Prevent Teen and Unplanned Pregnancy about 48 percent of pregnancies in the United States are unplanned. And while the teen pregnancy rate has gone down, what is going up is the unplanned pregnancy rate among women in their twenties and thirties.

So that settles it. There are a lot of parents out on the singles market, but some stigma still exists when it comes to dating someone who started their family before they met you. So should you?

Single parents, despite being parents now, are still people who live, love and seek companionship. If you meet someone who shares your values and your personalities mesh, if you both meet each other's emotional needs—go for it! Get to know each other just as you would if you were both single without kids. But keep in mind that as you both go charging into the romantic field—there's a little someone else there who has a stake in it.

The kid. Ask yourself, the childless looking to date someone with a child:

Do you like kids? I hope so, because you're about to encounter one if things get serious.

But you shouldn't meet that kid yet. Although you should be wary if someone you date is in a rush for you to meet and be around their child. Children, who tend to respond strongly—whether in the positive or negative—to the friends or romantic partners of their parents, shouldn't be exposed early or often to new people in their parents' lives. If someone is in a rush for you to bond with their child it suggests a severe immaturity on the behalf of the person you're dating. Their focus should be on getting to know you and protecting their kid from disappointment if it turns out that their kid likes you, but they—over time—don't. The kid won't understand why you broke up with them too when you fell out with their mom or dad.

But wait? How old is that kid? If the child is older, like say you're dating a thirtysomething and his or her child is over the age of eight and things start to get serious, you will have to contend with a child who has lived the last near decade of his or her life without you, might not be all that impressed with you and has their own well-formed thoughts and opinions on things. If the child is younger, like a toddler or infant, that may bring up a host of other concerns—like will your partner have time to spend with you when the child is so small and helpless? When was the last time your partner was with the mother or father of the baby? How long have they been broken up? Are you just a rebound if it hasn't been that long? Is it likely they'll get back together? Or are they desperate for someone to help raise their kid and be their companion, a sort of "instant family" situation for the childless?

Older kids need less attention or supervision but can get attached or be very vocal in their dislike. Younger kids still require a lot of their parents' attention, are largely helpless and may come with the baggage of a potentially unresolved, recently ended relationship. Many times the only children who won't affect who you date are "adult" children if you're dating a significantly older partner. (And even those children are often very opinionated about who their parents date.)

Expectations. People who already have kids typically don't have time for a lot of pie-in-the-sky "filler." Meaning, they want to know how serious (or not serious) you are pretty quickly and in that honesty, a romantic truth can be found that could easily benefit both parties. People with kids know what they (and ideally their kid) want and need—and tend to be blunt about it, especially in the case of single mothers. While they still love romance, most have gotten over abstract, unrealistic romantic notions that aren't moored in any reality and are focused on what is tangible in a relationship. That directness cuts down quite a bit on the flirty confusion that often arises with carefree singles who have more than enough time to obsess over whether someone likes or "like likes" you.

For those on the other side, moms and dads out in the dating market, it's also important for you as well to remember your kids are the priority. Their needs, safety and comfort are more important than a new boyfriend or girlfriend. Any new person in your life has to go through the initial checklist. Any change in your status—from never dating to seriously dating—must be addressed with the kid(s) in mind.

1. If your children are old enough to understand, you should let them know beforehand that you plan to start dating and what that means for your fam-

ily. The conversation should be frank and age appropriate. The kids don't need to know the nitty-gritty details, but they do need to understand what you're doing, why and how this will potentially affect them.

2. Once you meet someone you like, run them through your initial checklist. Who are they? What are their intentions? Does he have kids? Does he like kids? Is this serious? How well do you know him? How long have you dated? Is this heading toward marriage? If you don't know the answer to even one of these, you should probably hold off on introducing who you're dating to your child.

Quite a few of my childless clients weren't all that interested in dating someone with kids. Sure, some said they would, potentially, if the person was the right person (never say never), but it wasn't a preference, and that's understandable. A child complicates things because, as I stated before, the child should come first. Being able to just drop everything to go out, the amount of time they have to invest in dating, availability, have those getting-to-know-you and other bond-building conversations are all issues when dating someone with a child. Because all dates and conversations can be preempted or canceled due to "kid issues."

Other issues:

Lack of patience: As I'm finding out with my toddler son, children require a zenlike level of tolerance at times. They're young, still learning and still developing their social skills. So if the occasional temper tantrum, accident or crying fit sounds unappealing to you, dating with kids will be difficult.

Who has custody: Whoever is the primary caretaker for the child is the one who will have less time to devote to the relationship.

Baby mama (and daddy) drama: This depends on how healthy the relationship is between the parents of the child. If they get along well and are relatively content, any complications may be minimal. If hurt feelings and anger are still being thrown about, you may have wandered into an emotional war zone you never wanted.

Discipline and familial roles: Once you start to spend time with the child, things can get complicated quickly. What will the child call you—person who is not his or her mother or father? If the child is rude or hurtful or misbehaves, how do you discipline them? If you disagree with how the child is being raised, how do you voice those concerns? This is where those communication and conflict resolution skills really come in handy. You and your partner should discuss all of this before you start spending time with the child. Preset the rules and even if you have permission to act as an authority figure with the child, keep in mind that you still aren't that child's parent—yet. Not until you've committed to the family.

Marrying an individual versus marrying a family: They're not your kids, but if things get serious, they might be. And if you're single—untouched by familial duties—you will inherit an instant family when you marry or move in with someone with kids.

Don't take it personally: Did the kid yell at you? Say they hate you? Shout, "You're not my father?" Suck it up. They're a kid and they're still growing and learning. It might take a while for them to adjust to your presence. Children are adaptable. Over time, once they realize you're here to stay, they will likely warm up. Especially if you keep communication open and work on issues like family duties and discipline in a fair way with the parent.

It can be tough for a single person to date someone with kids, as the single person may not be as sensitive or understanding of the time constraints. This is why of those I've counseled who already have children I've found they've preferred to date other singles who also have children. But even in those cases, you still need to talk to your kids, you still need to take your time before introducing the children to each other or your partner. It's always "proceed with caution" when you have a child because it's not just you who will be impacted if your partner moves in, or you marry or you break up. Your child will be affected as well.

Because partners come and go. Kids are forever. Date accordingly.

Let's take a run through the checklist!

- Have you and your partner been dating for more than six months to a year?

- Has the relationship reached a point of seriousness where it could eventually lead to either cohabitation or marriage?

- Has your partner made clear their intentions toward you—and your family?

- Has your partner expressed a desire or appreciation for what children bring to a relationship?

- Does your partner have a healthy idea of what a family is? Of what parenting is?

- Does your partner respect the bond you have with your child and the time you need to dedicate to them?

- Have you and your partner talked
  about what your child will call them
  if they start to take on a larger role in
  both your lives?

The better you know the person you're dating, the more secure you can feel in introducing your child to them. Again, delay introduction until you're sure about your new partner. Children get attached quickly and don't like change. If you're introducing someone new to their lives make sure it's someone with a strong chance of going the distance.

CHAPTER 17

Know When to Fold 'Em

Lana would probably be an ideal serial monogamist if it weren't for the fact that in her multiple, lengthy relationships she'd always hoped for marriage.

There was Alex, who she met right after college—her first love. He was smart, handsome, charmingly awkward and Peter Pan–esque. But that "boy who never grew up" nature wore thin as years passed without a marriage proposal. Lana was planning their future children and wondering about the wedding when Alex had long ago decided he only wanted to be friends with Lana and wasn't ready to settle down at twenty-five.

But Alex didn't want to be "the bad guy" to

dump his girlfriend, so he let the relationship last a good seven years and two apartments before she caught him cheating, leading to her dumping him.

It took Lana years to get over Alex—who she is friends with now, but wasn't on speaking terms with for almost a decade. After Alex, Lana—then in her thirties—met Vincent and was swooped up in a grand, whirlwind love affair of weekend getaways, vacations, executive suites in hotels and romantic dinners. She was madly in love, convinced Vincent was her soul mate, as they both never seemed to tire of each other or their conversation. There was an insatiable passion in the relationship that was frighteningly intense. And unlike the boyish Alex, Vincent was "a man's man"—mature, serious, strong and confident. There was really only one problem—Vincent was married.

Lana was Vincent's mistress for most of her thirties, caught up in the excitement of the affair to the exclusion of her desire to get married and have kids. The relationship eventually ended when Lana realized that Vincent could never support her—emotionally or financially—as his priority was always his wife and their son. Vincent, who said he was staying with his wife for their child, didn't see divorce as an option, and Lana realized she'd again wasted her time.

Heartbroken but resolute Lana walked away

from a near decadelong affair to being in her forties with the goal of finding a husband and settling down. But now the dates were fewer and further in-between. Her most recent two-year relationship involving a younger man with three kids had fallen apart after she discovered numerous infidelities. And now she was single, forty-seven, childless and wondering where all the time had gone.

Nearly all of Lana's friends had married. Most had children or had adopted. She found herself enraged. How had this happened?

But if she was honest with herself, she knew. She could rail over Alex or damn Vincent, but the fact remained—once she realized there was no future that looked like marriage, instead of cutting her losses, Lana held on to hope that these relationships would pay off and she would prove herself wrong.

But she never did. Her gut told her these relationships were dead ends, but her heart soldiered on.

Now, facing a potentially childless future, Lana hopes to meet someone who already has children for her to dote on and help raise. Men who aren't serious don't get second and third looks. But it didn't have to be this way.

Wanting is not the same as having. If your goal is marriage and family don't waste years on relationships that will never turn into that.

No matter what you do, if he or she still hasn't

made up their mind that you're "the one" after at least two or three years, you're never going to be "the one."

If Lana had listened to her gut, she would have noticed that her relationships with both Alex and Vincent were full of obvious deal breakers. Alex was immature, didn't want to have children and didn't believe in monogamy. In his early twenties he hadn't felt comfortable admitting that to his then-girlfriend, but by the time he was twenty-four, after they'd dated for three years, he knew he didn't want to marry Lana. Maybe in another decade he'd feel differently. But at twenty-four, marriage seemed like such an "adult" thing to do and that was all Lana wanted. She'd only had two boyfriends as an adult and he'd only had one girlfriend—but while she was satisfied, he desired to date more, feeling he'd lost out on a lot of fun in his twenties by being with Lana. He knew he was wrong to cheat on her, wrong to drag the relationship out when he knew it was over three years into it, but again, his immaturity made him want to avoid their problems rather than confront them.

Vincent was married. Divorce was never on the table. He pursued Lana even though he knew he could never commit to her, and Lana continued in the relationship for most of her thirties because she'd become so attached to Vincent romantically. She was in love with him and with that love came a naïve hope that drastically colored her judgment. It took her years to realize the love she felt so passionately about would only lead to pain.

Lana wanted love. Like most of us do. But what she did with both Alex and Vincent was "settle." She'd stopped paying attention to the "he'll never marry me" reality and got caught up in the Hollywood packaged, fairy-tale logic that "true love conquers all," and beasts can be turned into princes if you're just willing to sacrifice your twenties and thirties—your prime baby-making years—to them.

But it wasn't worth it. It never is if your goal is to get married. If you're not engaged or talking about marriage after dating for two years, what's the holdup? And why do I say only two years instead of four or ten?

You already know each other: After two years you two should know each other pretty well. Your likes, dislikes, whether you want kids and when, and—most important—whether this relationship is leading to marriage. He or she should be talking about it, dropping hints or addressing it head-on. And if the prospect of matrimony makes them shout, "Change the subject" you already know you're not getting married.

But you still have concerns: After two years you know what your partner's flaws are and whether you can handle them. So are the flaws something you laugh off or are they "fatal" relationship-killing flaws you hope, pray and beg will go away? Are you hoping that if you hang in there time will cure immaturity, a temper, chronic cheating, lying, poor money management, no desire for family, selfishness, abusive or controlling behavior—you may be wasting your time. People grow older and wiser, but if something is at the core of their being, it won't change. If his way of dealing with his crippling insecurities is to mock you until you burst into tears, that probably won't stop even if he does marry you.

Once you've hit the two-year threshold and nothing's changed—the problems are still glaring problems, your partner still has no interest in marriage—you have to determine why you're staying with this person. If you don't care whether you get married and you're happy with the relationship, go for it. Continue on that way. But if you want to get married, this is a clash of values. Meaning, you value marriage, but your partner doesn't. Eventually not being married will breed resentment and distrust. Because why would the person you love not want to share in something you value so dearly? It would become a hurtful rejection that would turn into a poisonous anger.

You can't just settle unless you're planning on settling for disaster.

Be honest about what you want: You want marriage? Make that the priority. Those who don't want marriage, no matter how sweet or nice, are no-goes. As in, it's better to end it sooner rather than years later when you're in love and deeply attached. While it might hurt to be temporarily single, it'll hurt more when a decade has gone by and you're still not where you want to be romantically.

Be honest about what your partner wants: When your partner tells you they don't want kids, don't want to get married, don't want you to move, believe them.

Stop auditioning: Remember "auditioning," that fatal dead-end relationship trait from chapter 12 about psychological projection? You can be the best you possible. You can be a great helpmate and partner. You can pay for every meal and wash all the laundry, but if they don't want to marry you there is no amount of good behavior that can turn this relationship around. They don't want to get married. It's not that they're lying and if they just finally see how good you are they'll come around. They're not coming around.

Face the facts: If he or she is abusive, controlling, violent or pathologically selfish, if they have substance abuse problems, if they can't be faithful and you value monogamy, why are you putting yourself through this? Why do you want someone so much the antithesis of your values in your life, let alone married to you?

Set them free: When it's going nowhere, even if you love them, for the sake of you both, you need to be apart so that you are both open and available for someone else who might better fit your wants and needs. When you've reached a point of impasse, end the relationship with grace and understanding. Remember that even though you're hurt because you wanted marriage, you both chose to be in the relationship despite your concerns. You're both adults. End things in a mature and clean way, forgive and let go. You don't want to carry the hurt and disappointment from your no-go love into your next relationship.

Lana, when pressed, admits that in the years she spent with Alex and Vincent there were other men who had liked her, loved her, but she'd ignored them because she was committed to men who would not commit to her. Notice the irony in that statement— she missed out on the possibility of marriage and a family because she was busy trying to get those two things out of Peter Pan and a married guy. A boy who couldn't grow up and a man who could never commit to her. She'd had her fun, and she'd had her romance, but where was her commitment? Where was her marriage? Where was her family?

You can't meet the one you want if you're still involved with someone who won't commit to you. Love could be out there waiting, looking for you while you fret over how you can win over what can never be won. Cutting your loses is a difficult but necessary part of dating. Not every relationship is going to end in wedding bells. But if that's the goal, you can't spend a lot of time on people who won't pay off at the altar. We simply have to get better at recognizing romantic disaster before we go charging into it headfirst.

Knowing when to let go is an important part of love.

Go down the checklist to see if you (or your partner) are already one foot out the door.

- You or your partner no longer feels like your emotional needs are being met in the relationship.

- Communication has become difficult to the point of mostly fighting or not talking at all.

- You want to change your partner or your partner is trying to change you.

- You are constantly comparing your partner to others.

- One side feels it is putting more into the relationship and is doing more compromising than the other.

- You no longer feel good about yourself or your partner in the relationship.

- You don't like who you've become in the relationship.

- You or your partner has become hyper critical and micromanaging.

- You or your partner no longer looks forward to spending time together.

Love changes just as we change with age, experience and time. While some relationships are forever, some are just for a season. Accept that and know love accordingly.

CHAPTER 18

The Butt Pads Have to Come Off

Patricia Highsmith's 1955 novel *The Talented Mr. Ripley* tells the story of Tom Ripley, an ambitious young man who conceals his true intentions and feelings in order to manipulate what he wants out of people. His entire life is an untold lie and the ending of the novel (and the 1999 film version of it) is a continuation of that lie. He never gets real. He never emotionally invests. And the consequences are isolation and constant fear of the truth eventually getting out. He can never let anyone get close, lest they learn his terrible secret. Highsmith ends the novel with her antagonizing protagonist wondering, "was he going to see policemen waiting for him on every pier that he ever approached?"

In our pursuit of love, we meet quite a few Tom Ripleys. Sometimes it's even us who don the mask that obscures how we really think and feel. Usually we do this out of some deep-seated insecurity that who we are isn't enough for love. And by saying that who we are isn't enough, I mean that this isn't a matter of buying clothes that fit or practicing making eye contact. This is about feeling that—at our core—we don't deserve love because of who we are at that same core. So we put on an illusion of self that we live in fear of being called on.

We hide, hoping we never get caught. We never get close because getting close to someone would defeat the purpose of such a deception. These acts—ranging from fear of commitment and emotional detachment to lying about serious "deal breaker" issues in what may affect the perception of your value on the dating market—all eventually lead to disappointment.

Whether you're bad with communicating, bad with money or bad when you're not sober—at some point you have to deal with these issues honestly with those you are romantically pursuing. Otherwise—what's the point? Love is supposed to bring us closer. Hiding and lies push us apart, especially when, to "lure" those we desire to us, we trap them with self-defeating tactics.

Self-defeating tactics like these take many forms:

- Lying about your age, race, looks or gender in an online profile

- Lying about your education or profession

- Lying about wealth, talents or abilities

- Exaggerating our past relationships or accomplishments

- Being afraid to meet people in person after talking to them at length online

But not all of the things we hide or try to manipulate are lies meant to enhance our standing—others are intricate parts of ourselves we hide out of fear of rejection or prejudice.

Such as:

- Your true sexual orientation

- Poor financial background

- HIV or other sexually transmitted disease status

- Mental health history

- Past drug or alcohol addiction

- Criminal background

- A change in identity or gender reassignment

- Your complicated "situation" (divorced, married but separated, still living with ex, living at home with your parents, etc.)

Even though some of these things come with a real negative bias or prejudice, being able to hide them while in a relationship is not realistic. If your goal is love, at some point you have to start being real. You have to come out from behind your emotional walls and barriers, from behind your elaborate online profile and be your true self. Don't construct an elaborate fantasy for yourself online that falls apart the minute you open your mouth or show your face. Authenticity, letting someone like you for you, will lead to better relationships and a better dating experience in the long run.

Even if, initially, it looks insurmountable.

Understanding why we choose these lies begins with understanding fear. We all go through some point in our lives where we experience a rejection that severely distorts our view of ourselves. That rejection breeds a fear, "if they know me, they won't like me," that turns into a questioning of self, "what is it about me that makes me so unlikable? Who am I?" Dissatisfied with who we are, we find ourselves desiring the lives of others, then we distort ourselves in order to become what we desire.

We think that by doing this we will finally get the love we want, but that's a dangerous illusion. No love can be built on a foundation of lies. No bond can be maintained that was forged on a false pretense.

Yet it's this fear that causes us to question everything in an effort to get love, to set up self-sabotaging roadblocks that keep us from it.

Who are you fooling? Someone who doesn't like him- or herself will come across as unlikable in the end.

And yet lying is pretty prevalent in the dating world, now made even easier online. A recent Ok-Cupid survey took a look at the biggest lies some of their users typically engaged in. Men who claimed to be six feet tall tended to actually be two inches shorter than that, at 5'10". People typically claim to make 20 percent more money than they actually earn. Of the pictures they post, they tend to be "older" pictures, in some cases from years ago—often revealing a fitter, thinner and younger-looking person than they are today. Most users who identify as bisexual largely only message members of the same gender with frequency.

Some of these lies may be forgivable. (Particularly in the areas of height or wealth if the exaggerations aren't too drastic.) But others—like using your basic training photo when you were ripped at twenty-five as your profile photo when you are presently forty and obese—are unacceptable. Because what's the endgame? Is it just to get a lot of messages online, or is it to actually go on dates? Because if your profile description is so far off base that your potential date wouldn't even recognize you if you met in person, you've gone too far.

But other issues—like mental health or STD status—are understandably difficult to address. Even if you're honest about your battle with depression or lupus, that's not something you want to put on your profile or disclose on a first date. Still, if the goal is to find a relationship and build trust, you have to find the right time to tell.

Weigh the pros and cons: While it's not worth telling every date about that time you spent two days in jail for forging checks while in the midst of a manic episode, if you're starting to get serious, have been seeing each other for longer than six weeks and think the relationship has potential, now might be the time to start testing the waters for self-disclosure.

What about trust?: When you tell the person you're dating something that possibly even your own mother doesn't know about you, trust is big. Just as it's important for you to self-disclose your potential deal breakers, it's important to determine if you can trust the person you're dating. Take time—six to eight weeks—to get to know who you're dating, learn their values and see if they're someone who would be understanding.

Are you dating a bigot? There are some things about ourselves we can't do all that much about—like if you do suffer from mental health issues. So it makes little sense to pursue a relationship once you discover the person you're dating has a deep-seated hatred/fear of the mentally ill. The same goes for if who you're dating is homophobic and transphobic and you were born a man but live as a woman. Or if you're biracial but look one race more than the other, and the person you're dating "assumes" you're white or Asian, not realizing you have a parent of another race that they are prejudiced against.

Don't wait until it's "too late": While it's technically never too late to come clean, once feelings get involved and you drop a deal breaker issue on your partner, things can get ugly fast. Disclosing one lie will lead to a questioning, then unraveling, of every part of the relationship. Again, Hollywood has lied to you. Most people don't just "get over it" due to the "power of love" when they find out you've been stalking them for months or that you dramatically changed your identity and lied about who your parents were or that you were just pretending to be a high school student for a journalism assignment. Once your big story gets out, you're less likely to win someone's love and more likely to end up with a broken heart and restraining order.

Assess the situation—both yours and theirs: Some things you should disclose immediately and honestly—like if you are a trans man or woman, if you are bisexual and had past long-term relationships with someone of the same gender, if you are recently divorced or have young kids, if you don't drink alcohol—ever. Other things can wait a bit, like if that reason you never drink alcohol is because you're in recovery for alcoholism. And with others still, it's more of a "wait and see" approach, like broaching your mental illness, past treatable physical ailments or messy financial or legal history. Waiting to self-disclose may actually improve your chances of acceptance in some cases—like waiting before going into depth about your painful divorce or discussing how you suffer from depression but have been on medication and have been stable for years. The thing is to know the difference between what is willfully misleading and therefore a malicious lie, and what is private that can only be disclosed after a sufficient amount of trust has been built up.

In the end, though, with everything, our best course of action is honesty. If you don't have to lie, if you don't have to pretend, you know who truly likes you for you. You know where you stand and you don't run the risk of creating pain in relationships that were never going to work out.

Getting real about who you are is key—in life and love. If you want to be accepted you have to conduct yourself in an acceptable manner.

Get out the pad, get out the pen (or the laptop and your fingers) and get to work on this exercise:

- Make a list of your best qualities.

- Make a list of your flaws.

- Make a list of words to describe yourself.

- Write down four things you'd like to improve about yourself.

- Afterward, take the list to friends and family you have trusting relationships with to go over why you wrote down what you did and get their input on whether they feel your views of yourself match their own.

- Compare notes between these outside observers and your own initial findings.

Another neat group exercise is for everyone to write one positive thing and one critique about other members of the group, without putting down who said what, then present the differing opinions to each member of the group. Afterward, each person reads what the others in the group thought of them out loud and all discuss whether these views were right or wrong and why someone may have written what they did.

CHAPTER 19

There's No Difference Between Your
Brain in Love and Your Brain on Drugs

It was just supposed to be a "sometimes" thing between Jack and Christa.

They were friends—but friends with "benefits."
And those benefits meant that while they were both
single, they enjoyed a friendship coupled with occasional sex. But what was occasional began to occur
more and more often, and before she had a chance to
fully understand what was happening, Christa
couldn't stop thinking about Jack.

The same Jack who for years she thought was too
immature, too irresponsible and too goofy for her
more serious tastes was now always at the forefront

of her mind. She found herself missing him when he wasn't around, even though when they were around each other (and not having sex) they probably spent more time being slightly frustrated with each other than anything else. Jack, after all, was a joker. He used humor as a defense mechanism to mask his real feelings. He joked constantly and maybe, back when they first became friends, Christa thought he was funny. But now when he made jokes at her expense they stung. They made her cry. They started fights.

Before Jack knew it, he and Christa were in a relationship that from the outside it seemed like Christa hated, but her emotions were strong and when he tried to end it she became near hysterical. How did they go from being friends to this? And how did Christa find herself in love with a man she had written off years ago as "just a friend"?

Did Jack become all that more lovable or was this just Christa's brain on drugs—love drugs?

Let's consult the experts—top-selling pop singers.

When pop star Ke$ha first performed on NBC's long-standing live sketch comedy show *Saturday Night Live* in 2010, most people couldn't get over how nervously bad the performance appeared to be. (And knowing the reputation of the singer, there's some reason to believe it was bad on purpose.) But I was captivated by something else entirely. While I can't really attest to being the target audience for her style of overprocessed, electric acid Kool-Aid party pop, one thing stood out. She performed a song she penned called "Your Love Is My Drug" where she croons through a computer about her judgment "getting kinda hazy" and her "steeze [becoming] affected" if she keeps acting like a "lovesick crackhead."

This will probably be the first (and the last) time I reference Ke$ha lyrics in my work, but this bit of disposable pop has a point. There's not that much difference from falling in love and taking mescaline—both (for a little while anyway) will get you high.

Ke$ha isn't the only one to notice similarities between love and chemical dependency. Toni Braxton sang "You're Makin' Me High" back in 1996, just like singer Robert Palmer called for the doctor in his "Bad Case of Loving You" in 1978, and funk/soul group Bloodstone sang of love taking them to the sky on "Natural High" in 1973. Love and drugs are prime romantic real estate in music due to how the same mental receptors that "reward" us with a pleasant sensation (typically a rush of dopamine or oxytocin) when we do something that makes us feel good are the same chemicals that are overloaded when we're intoxicated . . . and are the same feelings that give love that addictive feeling.

Think back to the last time you got your heart broken, the last time you went from seeing the one you loved every day to hardly ever or never at all. Think of the feelings you went through to get over a particularly intense relationship and ask yourself if any of the emotions and desperate actions I list below have a familiar ring to you?

- Feeling like you need to see the person you loved daily or even several times a day

- Finding yourself going back to the relationship over and over, failing at ending the relationship or accepting that it's over

- Doing whatever you can—lying, begging, bargaining—to keep the relationship going

- Spending money and time on the relationship to the detriment of all other relationships including friends and family

- Doing risky things to try to get the one you love back

- Focusing more and more time and energy staying in the relationship or trying to get it back

- Feeling euphoric when you're together but depressed when you're apart

- Feeling depressed once the relationship ends

- Loss of inhibitions and judgment when in the relationship

If you saw any of yourself in the list above, you've been in love. You've also been an addict. That list was rewritten and modified from several "Are you an addict?" and "What are the symptoms of drug withdrawal?" checklists used by health professionals. Just like pop singers have done, I just switched out all references to drugs and changed it to it being about a person.

A person who is your drug.

There's a science behind love and sex. Understanding it helps us make better decisions about our relationships—which ones are good to pursue and which ones are chemically dependent dead ends.

In the love and neuroscience study anthropologist Helen Fisher conducted for her book *Why We Love*, she found that in our brains there is a reward system for romance. Among those who participated in her study, when individuals who'd recently fallen in love saw pictures of their significant others, their brains lit up in MRIs in the same way brains using drugs or experiencing something desirable would.

And those surveyed spoke emphatically of how they'd die for the ones they loved. Of how they felt euphoric in their romance. There was a biological imperative for love, per Fisher, no different from our drive for water, food, safety or shelter. We're supposed to want it so badly.

"People live for love, they kill for love, they die for love, they sing about love," Fisher told CNN in 2006.

And other studies and research have backed Fisher's claims.

Kayt Sukel chronicles how brain chemistry affects attraction in her 2012 book *Dirty Minds*, and writes how just the right "picture, smell or song can evoke commanding memories, along with any emotions behind them."

Love stems from our minds, not our hearts—which are much too busy pumping oxygen-filled blood through our veins to be bothered with our romantic machinations. So the same places that hold our centers of logic rule over that most illogical of things—falling in and out of love.

Once you understand that love chemicals can sometimes leave you in the lurch, you can better modify your behavior or even avoid perilous situations. For instance, if you're in a purely sexual relationship with someone for recreation, don't be surprised if over time you unwittingly begin to fall for them. The same goes for particularly intense and intimate friendships where one party falls in love while the other doesn't. The familiarity, the constant interaction, that chemical reward system in our heads, associates the dopamine and oxytocin released with the person we are having sex with or spending so much time with.

But it goes even further than that with our brains. Many studies have shown that women can detect whether a man has an immune system that is different from her own—and possibly more comparable to hers—by his smell. Often these experiments involve having women of child-bearing age smell shirts men have worn, sans deodorant and scented soaps or lotion. When women remarked that one shirt smelled better than another, it was often found that the women had selected shirts belonging to men who had much more varied immune system profiles from their own. The more diverse a mother and father's immune systems are, the more likely they are able to produce healthy offspring. But even odder than that, in 2008 a study was published in the Royal Society's scientific journal *Proceedings B* that found that women taking oral contraceptives, or birth control pills, could not "sniff" out the difference and sometimes actually preferred the scent of those men whose immune systems were less varied and more similar to their own.

Biologists theorized that the hormones in birth control simulate a feeling of pregnancy in a woman's body, which may dampen sex drive, impact a woman's sense of smell or make her suddenly prefer the company of relatives—or those with similar immune systems to her own—instead of a more varied partner. Potentially, when a woman stops taking birth control, she may find she suddenly doesn't like how her partner smells all that much.

And would prefer the company of someone with a little variety in their DNA.

All this again points to the fact that love is habit-forming. With familiarity, with time, with sexual contact, with or without hormones manipulated by birth control, we can find biology playing a role in our love life. While it may seem kismet, behind the scenes, deep in the recesses of your mind—it may not be.

But don't be too surprised if you find that, at times, you can't tell the difference.

Sometimes we find ourselves attached to people we're not sure are right for us. The feelings seem to come from nowhere and we wonder—are we just in love with the notion of love?

Ask yourself this:

- Is there a "deal breaker" flaw, a non-starter issue that I always knew was present but I think the issue will resolve itself or go away, even though that's not logical?

- Was the relationship initially born out of a hookup situation where we rarely, if ever, dated?

- When I try to visualize our relationship in the future do I realize it's hard to see us together?

- When I take sex off the table, do I find that we have no other things that are compatible or no shared values?

- Do I find myself expecting things of my partner that early on in the relationship I either had no opinion about or didn't care?

- Do I feel incomplete if I'm not in a relationship?

- When I'm not in a relationship do I feel anxious and question my self-worth?

- Do I define myself by who I'm with?

- Do I change my personality, even my beliefs, to fit in better with my partner?

- Do I know that I deserve better—more love or support or affection—from my partner but am too afraid to confront them about it for fear they will leave me?

- When I feel sad or anxious and I reach out to my partner for support, does it feel like they reject me more than comfort me?

Love isn't supposed to hurt. Love isn't supposed to make us feel disrespected and used. Learn the difference and cut ties with those who don't appreciate you.

CHAPTER 20

You Can't Direct Change, but You Can Inspire It

The Greek story of Pygmalion tells of a sculptor who falls in love with his inanimate creation. He devotes hours to this figure of a woman he has crafted, buying her gifts and looking upon her longingly, and for his devotion he is eventually rewarded by the gods of ancient Greece, who bring the sculpture to life.

There are so many stories like this in our mythology, our shared history, our fiction as human beings, that it shouldn't be surprising that so many of us wed ourselves to the notion that we can change what we cannot control. That if we simply devote ourselves and give all of ourselves unselfishly to a task we will be rewarded.

Sometimes we want something so badly, we want to make it real. But that's not how love works.

Many people—male and female—believe they can enter a relationship with someone who is not "100 percent" and make them whole. Maybe they have insecurities or a substance abuse problem. Maybe they have family woes or struggle with depression. Maybe they're angry—a lot. Maybe they struggle with low self-esteem, poor body image or familial woes. Maybe they aren't educated. Maybe they aren't sophisticated.

Maybe you pity them and feel like they never had a good shot.

But your love can't change them.

There is no amount of love that can make a person do what they don't want to do. And I'm not talking about small things—like how someone may dress or their manners (although those things also cannot change without the person being willing to learn)—but major concerns, like the belief that if your partner doesn't want children you can convince them that they actually do. The belief that you can change your partner's values to match your own, in spite of their personality or background.

You can't make someone change. But you can try

to inspire change in your own example. You can try to influence. But true change always comes from within.

First, you have to recognize the behavior your partner is exhibiting that you don't like and wish would change. Is that behavior something that is dangerous to them or you—such as a substance abuse problem or an anger issue? Or is it something more emotional, like they have a tendency to shut down or withdraw when facing difficult situations? Or is it regarding infidelity, lingering insecurity or low self-esteem? If it is dangerous behavior, change may be difficult, as in these situations your partner has to reach a point where they realize what they are doing is inadvertently impacting the relationship in an unhealthy fashion. They may need to seek therapy or treatment but are reluctant to accept their flaws. While it might help a partner struggling from alcohol abuse for you to stop drinking, that won't cure them of their addiction. Only therapy and hard work from within themselves will. Other behaviors, like emotional ones that put stress on the relationship, may be a matter of seeking psychological therapy or couples therapy from a counselor. You could seek therapy to help you cope with your loved one's issues and later invite them to attend a session with you, where you can discuss the problems together.

Some issues we may wish to see our partner

change are about their being irresponsible, immature, inconsistent or rude—like perhaps your partner has a habit of making cruel or disparaging jokes, or of being vulgar or do things to embarrass or shame you in public. Maybe they're self-involved and forgetful and engage in harmful name-calling with you.

If your desire is for your partner to respect you and make the effort to curtail their more troublesome behaviors, you have to:

Address the issue directly: Don't sugarcoat it, but don't be unnecessarily rude. Clearly outline what the issue is, what impact it is having on the relationship, and ask if the partner is willing to negotiate for a happy medium or to modify his or her behavior.

Be a model: If your partner is rude, he or she may expect rudeness in return, as at some point they have learned that this is a way to communicate. But it's not healthy. Exhibiting the same disrespectful behavior will not change anything. Be the change you want your partner to adopt by refusing to engage in hostile, disrespectful or negative conversations or activities. Respond to your partner's crudeness how you wish he or she would handle the situation, then demand that they do the same.

Stop saying, start doing: Sometimes we engage in threats or controlling behaviors in the hopes that they will "train" our partner. But our partner is not a dog who peed on the carpet. If they are a certain way (and have been that way for some time) no amount of rubbing their nose in it will curtail the behavior. Instead, find mature, responsible ways to respond to the bad behavior and to remove yourself from the situation. Be above the behavior. Again, lead by example in hopes that they will eventually do the same.

Make your points clear: If the behavior is a deal breaker that could end the relationship, be clear about that and hold firm. If they do something rude and your response is to remove yourself from the situation or refuse to engage, hold yourself to that response. Don't be inconsistent and reward bad behavior. Make it clear that you are hurt and that this hurt must be dealt with in a mature fashion. Real progress must be made, or you will continue to further remove yourself from the situation.

Be willing to let it go: We can't make someone change if they don't want to. If you find that your self-sacrifice, cajoling, praying and hoping is a fool's errand, you have to be willing to chalk this up to "life experience" and move on. Don't look at it like you failed, but that you and this person simply were not a good fit for the long haul. This doesn't mean you were wrong to love this person or to pursue the relationship, but sometimes there is no way to reconcile what has become irreconcilable.

Love is about acceptance. If you can't accept

something, then you may find you don't have a very stable love going with your partner. Your inability to accept something doesn't necessarily pinpoint a failure on your part but a realization that sometimes we're incompatible with others. Our hearts are in the right place, but our values aren't, as we discover that wanting, needing and having are all very different things.

You may want and desire your flawed partner, but you may find you don't need the dysfunction that comes with their bad behavior. You may have this person in your life as your own and relish the fact that you are not alone, but having doesn't equal happiness. There's no promise that you will be happier with someone than you would be if you were alone, regardless of compatibility.

Also, remember that sometimes when we find ourselves making excuses for our partner's bad behavior or our obvious incompatibilities—hoping that something changes—it is because we are not accepting reality. We have not accepted that the things we thought were true were never true. There were signs and signals along the way, and rather than deal, we chose to ignore them and hope we were wrong. We tried to flip it only to fall flat. This is a facet of projection, which we discussed in chapters 12 and 17, and projection isn't healthy because it keeps us from dealing with the reality of our situations.

Don't fall for the "type hype" in your head, making you try to force your square partner into a round hole. You are not Pygmalion and you did not create the one you loved from clay. You cannot wish for the change that will take him or her from "your type" to someone who shares your values.

You can't date disaster and think loving someone will make them change. Sometimes you have to let go.

When you think of your relationship, do you find these thoughts swirling in your head:

- On paper the person reads like my dream guy or girl, but I still feel insecure in the relationship.

- I feel I should want the relationship, but for some reason I'm not sure I understand, I don't.

- I hope that my partner will change, either through my actions or on their own.

- I hope that changes in career or having a child with my partner will change things for the better.

- I feel like something is "missing" in how we relate to each other.

- We look good together—and that's about it.

- We have great sexual chemistry, but

my partner is unreliable and inconsistent in their treatment of me.

- We don't have good sexual chemistry, but I feel the need to pretend like we do.

- I fear being single, but I also fear what will happen if I stay in this relationship.

- I fear what others will think if the relationship ends.

- They're such a catch and I think I'd must be crazy to not want them and stay with them—even though I know in my heart I don't want to be in the relationship anymore.

Expectations often color our perceptions. We can know something isn't right for us, but we'll still pursue it anyway—from either external or internal pressure—telling us our worth is not defined by ourselves but who we are with.

CHAPTER 21

You Can Fall in Love Again

In the James Cameron film *Titanic*, much is made of the passionate, once-in-a-lifetime love of Jack and Rose, played by a young Leonardo DiCaprio and Kate Winslet. Their meeting, her rescue by him from suicide and her promising to "never let go" as the ship sank, is the heart of the more-than-three-hour epic film. Yet, in the film, the older Rose went on from her young love and disaster to eventually marry, have a happy life and a family. Which is why the final image of the film, of a young again, ghost Rose reunited for all of eternity with Jack and the rest of those who perished in the disaster, was more disturbing to me than romantic.

One image, of Rose's life and new love, demonstrated that the intense romance of her youth filled her with the rigor and desire to live her life to the fullest. Including being open to a new love and having a family. So she would prefer an afterlife with a guy she only knew for a few days to the family she spent the rest of her adult life with? Sure, it hit the right romantic note for those caught up in that young love, but it didn't ring true. How could a fifty-plus-year life be inconsequential compared to what was, quite possibly, the worst night of her life when her whole world up to that point—her family, friends and her newfound love—all drowned in a frigid ocean?

But he was her "soul mate," says the teenage version of you from 1997. But this is adult you I'm talking to right now, and what are the chances that the boy or girl you loved at eighteen is the person you're married to now? What's the chance that in your late teens or early twenties you actually met your "soul mate"?

A "soul mate" is a scary prospect when you think of it.

It gives the impression that we only get one chance, one shot to make it right. And if we miss it, we miss it forever. There is no coming back. But that's not what life is like. We meet people. We date. We fall in love. We make a go for it. We either stay together or we fall apart. And if love ends, we mourn it, but we start over again. We move on. And we often continue to try, search and look for greater understanding and faith in each other. At the point of heartbreak it may feel like it's over, but it's never over.

My grandmother, like most of her generation, married young. With her husband she had four children, but later he was tragically killed in an accident. At the time, in the 1960s, being a widow or widower at any age was often looked at as a permanent thing. When your spouse died—the one you were supposed to be with, ideally until your own death—you weren't always expected to remarry. Or at least it was viewed as a difficult thing to do, especially since my grandmother already had four children. Yet she did remarry and go on to have two children with her second husband. For a myriad of reasons, this second marriage was actually healthier and stronger than the first that ended so abruptly. If my grandmother was more hung up on the notion of there only being one man for her, instead of getting on with the business of living her life, she might have missed out on a relationship that has been so dear to her.

It's not that the previous marriage was wrong, but starting over and being open to love is always right. We are not meant to have only one friend or one family member or one love for all time. We are meant to experience one another as part of humanity's family. We are meant to explore relationships, make connections and grow from them. Being with one person forever may work for some of us, but for others, perhaps love comes for a reason and a season and goes. And does that make their love worth less than those who stay together forty or fifty years? Whether you find love at twenty or at sixty-five, does it make a difference? Is the passion you feel not relevant? When we don't do things on some artificial schedule does it mean our loves are not real?

I had a best friend when I was fifteen. We stopped being friends when I was twenty. Does this mean I would never find another friend? Does that sound ridiculous to say, let alone type? If so, why do we view love this way?

If you love someone with all your heart and it doesn't work out, the next person you love isn't lesser or a consolation prize or leftover or accidental or a fluke. We have to stop looking at the human heart as if we only have so much love to give and we run out. Our love is an endless, renewable resource. We can lose love, then have our love renewed. It's not a fossil fuel you are burning out of the earth until you reach "peak love" and you have to ration it out. You don't have one child and have no love left over if you have a second. You don't have one friend, then decide you have no love left over for any new friends. You don't love a boyfriend or girlfriend or spouse, have that relationship end for whatever reason, then become banished to the National Home for Americans Who Wasted Their One Shot on Love.

We live and breathe and go on.

We need to stop fearing being hurt by love. While the pain stings and we cry and mourn, the end of love is something we can control no more than life and death. Losing love is part of life. And so is finding love again.

Although you may have been hurt in the past, it's far more likely that you will love again. All you have to do is let go of the notion that you are a failure if your loves haven't turned into forever, die two seconds after each other after sixty years of married love. If you love a person, any person, and it is valued and reciprocated, even if it ends, it was real.

Your feelings were real. And if you move on to love again, that love is real too. Embrace the chaos and uncertainty of life and adopt the mantra of those who have accepted that we change what we can change and accept what we cannot and pray that we will always know the difference between the two. Don't seek power over what we are powerless to control, and enjoy the ride.

Media mogul and talk show host Oprah Winfrey speaks a lot about the act of "surrender"—that point of giving yourself over to your beliefs, a higher power, to your inner faith and accepting the journey life sets in front of you. "God can dream a bigger dream for me, for you, than you can ever dream for yourself," Winfrey said. "When you've worked as hard and done as much and strived and tried and given and pled and bargained and hoped . . . surrender. When you have done all that you can do, and there's nothing left for you to do, give it up. Give it up to that thing that is greater than yourself, and let it then become a part of the flow."

As someone who dreamed of ending up on the couch of Oprah's iconic talk show, I found myself surrendering to the fact that I'd never get on there (her final season wrapped without my getting a spot), but through my own persistence and hard work, I ended up meeting Oprah anyway and interviewing her on my couch for a show I would later do on her OWN network, *Lovetown, USA*. By believing in my long-term plan—that dream of helping others find and keep love through my work as a matchmaker—my desires still found a way to come to fruition, albeit not in the way I'd initially envisioned.

In fact, in many ways, I did much better.

The same goes for love. Giving in to love and believing in your life plan for happiness may sound scary, but it's actually the most important step to finding and keeping the love you desire. We have to train our belief system by affirming our desires and abilities, and by toughing up our resolve against setbacks and rejection (seeing them for what they really are—lessons to prepare us for what we truly want). We must surround ourselves with likeminded and supportive individuals who affirm our gifts and resolve, learning to accept both compliments and constructive criticism, and, finally, if you're not feeling that confidence, fake it until you make it, instead. By living as one who believes, you will eventually become that person. You will be able to surrender and let go of fear.

Dating is an adventure—not a destination. Enjoy the things you can experience with each other and stop expecting the elaborate pageantry of some pumped-up dinner date designed by the fanciful expectations of modern theater and soap opera drama. Get out into the world with each other and experience new things. Go rock climbing. Take an art class together. See Shakespeare in the park. Have an adventure. Try something new. Learn something new about yourself and those you are with.

And stop letting the expectations of others weigh on you. The panic of friends and family on our relationship status at the expense of our deep and personal happiness is a burdensome drain. What are they so nervous and frightened for? We don't meet someone, court for a set period of time, stroll down a wedding aisle, have a "happily ever after," then quickly fade to black and roll credits. Our lives aren't complete with the exchanging of vows. They do not end with coupledom or matrimony. We have, as the old song goes "a lot of living to do." And we can do that together.

Marriage and a family aren't a means to an end

but part of a glorious beginning as our lives continue to grow, evolve, change and develop. To get fixated on these signposts of existence and believe you are incomplete or unimportant because you have not mastered them in some "traditional" sense is futile. What is traditional today wasn't traditional fifty years ago or a hundred years ago or a thousand years ago. Our society and the expectations that come with it are always changing. You can't put past expectations of courtship—rooted in a medieval context, when people died in their thirties—on our lives today where many of us thrive well into our sixties, seventies, eighties, nineties and beyond. Life is always changing and we shouldn't fear that. Because whether we want it to change or not, it most certainly will. Instead of wasting our time worrying about what we can't control, let's enjoy what we have and what there is here for us to experience and accomplish in the now.

Love is what we make it. You can enjoy the time you have here with the people who you desire and who value you, or you can spend a life of want, staring at greener hedges and bushes and pastures, chasing an endless rainbow for that pot o' golden wedding rings only to get there and wonder, "Now what?" It isn't about checking something off a list—it's about making a connection and living, loving to a natural conclusion. It's about being our best selves and experiencing it together. It is about not being afraid of living and not being afraid of love and all the wonderful strangeness that comes with it.

Stop looking at statistics. If you're hearing numbers about how 65 percent of black women aren't married, read between the lines and see that in actuality many of those studies count every black woman—from ages eighteen to sixty-five and beyond. It doesn't take into consideration that people delay marriage, that as we age many of us eventually marry, that divorce is part of our life, but so is cohabitation and marrying later in life and all the other wonderful ways we can come together and make lives and families. Stop punishing yourself and let go of the burden of expectation, of tradition, of family and society. Let go of timetables and checklists. Let go of perfection and the idea of there only being one path when there are so many dotting along the roadways of our life.

Let go and live your life.

Let go and let love rule.

Acknowledgments

Thank you, Jill. There are not enough words to express what you mean to me. My heart will forever be yours.

Thank you, Dad. You will always be my hero.

Thank you, Mom. I have never met a kinder spirit or gentler soul.

Thank you, Mr. & Mrs. C. Your love for each other served as an example I will never forget.

Thank you, Grandma and Grandpa Bright and Grandma and Grandpa Lewis. Thank you for your unconditional love, support and guidance. You are and always have been a major influence in my life.

Thank you, Carl. You unconditionally support me and unselfishly share your talents to help me succeed. I thank God for placing you in my life.

Thank you, Nikishia. Your constant support is more appreciated than you know.

Thank you, Carol, Alfred and Carolyn—my Sis-Sis, Bucky and Bunny.

Thank you, Andre Smith. No matter the ebb and flow of my life, you remain a constant, and I would not have it any other way. I always know you have my back.

Thank you, Yuson Charles. Your brilliance and persistence is electrifying. We have had a good ride, and what is scary is that we are just getting started.

Thank you, Rachel Greenwald. Your mentorship has allowed me to dream bigger than I ever have.

Thank you, Anthony Ross and Donae Thomas. You both are pure inspiration, and I think about you and pray for your dreams every day.

Thank you, Enver Yucel and family. You helped create a better version of me. I will forever be grateful.

Thank you, Danielle Wright-Fennell, Maia Blakenship and David Johns. No matter where the roads of life take us, I know we will forever be connected. Your support is priceless.

Thank you, Kailen Rosenburg. There is no one else I would rather travel this new path with. Our conversations remain etched in my mind.

Thank you, Lisa Hackner, Hilary Estey McLoughlin, Sheila Bouttier and Tomii Crump. You gave me confidence when I had none. I will never forget it.

Thank you, Oprah Winfrey, Sheri Salata, Erik Logan, Mashawn Nix, Endyia Kinney-Sterns and

Jessica Boyer. You helped me realize God can dream a bigger dream than I could ever imagine.

Thank you, Travers Johnson and the Gotham/Penguin family—William Shinker, Lisa Johnson, Lindsay Gordon, Casey Maloney, Spring Hoteling, Erica Ferguson and Lavina Lee. Your patience with me during this process is appreciated beyond words.

Thank you, family and friends. I am beyond grateful for the calls, messages, e-mails, and tweets of support I get on a daily basis. Whenever life gets tough, you have been there to hold me up.